There's History Around Every Bend

By Steve Procko and Kathy Thompson

Table of Contents

About the Cover: The Blue Ridge Scenic Railway near Murphy Junction
on its return trip from McCaysville/Copperhill to Blue Ridge.
Cover and Table of Contents photos by Steve Procko

Book layout & design by Steve Procko

Published by: There's History Around Every Bend, Ocala, Florida | HistoryBend.org

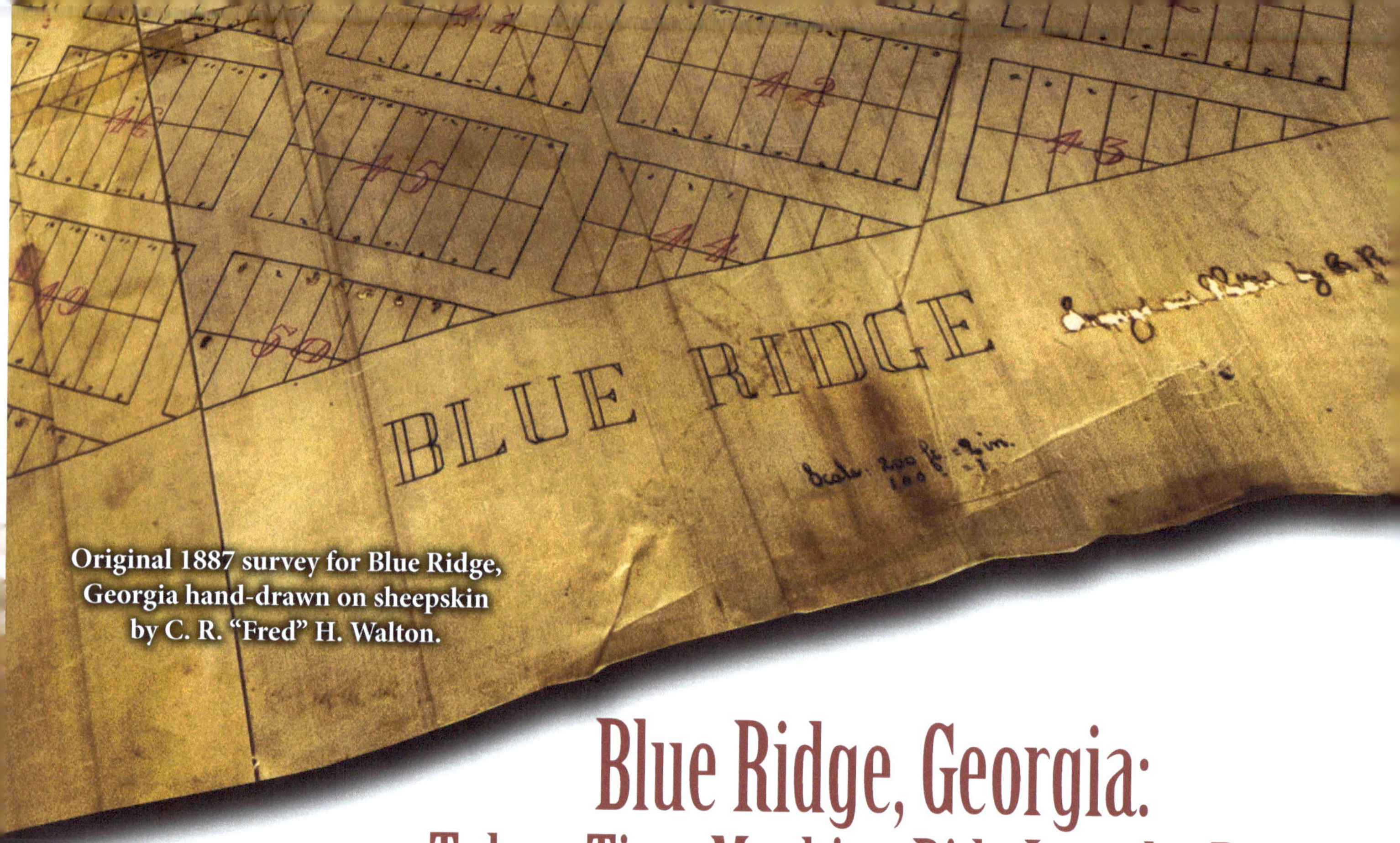

Original 1887 survey for Blue Ridge, Georgia hand-drawn on sheepskin by C. R. "Fred" H. Walton.

Blue Ridge, Georgia:
Take a Time Machine Ride Into the Past.
By Kathy Thompson

In comparison to other towns in the area, Blue Ridge is a relatively young and is not featured on the earliest maps of the region.

Prior to the establishment of Blue Ridge, other settlements such as Dial and Mineral Bluff (1840s), Morganton (1856), Epworth (1860s), and McCaysville (1870s), had already been founded and occupied by a small population of early settlers.

Fannin County was created from parts of Union and Gilmer Counties in 1854. The first map of Fannin County created in 1869 does not include Blue Ridge because it didn't exist yet.

Instead the map featured the county seat of Morganton surrounded by hundreds of 160-acre plats and their corresponding plat numbers, reminders of the 1832 Georgia Cherokee land lottery.

Circa 1890s - Blue Ridge, Georgia

One way to comprehend the historical evolution of the late-entry boom town is to visualize a mental journey back through time. Envision yourself seated on a log (your imaginary time machine) in the current downtown park of Blue Ridge.

You suddenly travel back to the early 1800s, where you find yourself deep within a thick, dense forest. Indigenous Cherokee villages are nearby along the Toccoa River and Fightingtown Creek near Epworth. You might occasionally spot lone individuals or small groups making their way between the settlements, but for the most part, solitude is your primary companion in this wilderness.

In the early 1880's, Mrs. H. C. Curtis tells you about the place that later became Blue Ridge:

"At that time it consisted of many acres of fallow land, covered with sage grass. There was only one house to be seen anywhere and that was the home of Elisha Green, and I believe it was located near where the County Court House now stands."

As time passes, the first settlers begin to arrive to places like Dial, Morganton and Epworth. Settlement is so heavy that in 1854 Morganton becomes the county seat of the newly formed Fannin County. But in the place where Blue Ridge would later be, you are alone.

The 1860s arrive and the Civil War breaks out. While no troops fought in this part of North Georgia, the Home Guard and Union sympathizers had violent, running confrontations, including a shoot-out in Morganton. But you are sitting on a log in today's city park and nothing is happening. The decade after the Civil War is a difficult one everywhere in Fannin County. The population dips as families move away. You are still alone.

"This superb locality was only a deserted sedge field, skirted by irregular knolls and flanked by the solitude of trackless forests where the restless Indian once roamed in primeval ascendancy. No visible signs of habitation greeted the eye of the tourist, save a settler's cabin on an adjacent hill."

- 1885 description of the desolation in the area that will become Blue Ridge.

After all your waiting, a tall bearded man named Michael "Mike" McKinney (1840-1925), Elisha Spencer "Spince" Green (1854-1926), and railroad surveyor/engineer, C. R. "Frank" H. Walton (Bef. 1860-1889) are wandering about. They are laying plans for a new town that they will name "Blue Ridge".

Mike knows there will be a town here, because he is largely responsible for routing the railroad in this direction, and he owns most of the land. It is 1885 and a population explosion is going to happen. You are about to have a lot of company.

The Mike McKinney family c1890s. Mike and his wife Hepsey are seated in the center. McKinney was largly responsible for determining the route of the railroad north of Ellijay.

Blue Ridge, Georgia; Circa 1900.

In the summer of 1886 the first locomotive arrives at the then "end of the line" located in the deserted sedge field that will soon become Blue Ridge. With steam billowing and the train whistle screaming, engineer William F. "Bill" Garwood (1869-1946) gives you a wave while leaning out the window of the cab at the rear of the firebox of the tiny locomotive named "Little Mary." '

Mike McKinney might be on the train or perhaps among the small group awaiting the train. Either way, he is relieved and satisfied; it has been a long and interesting challenge to bring the rails so far north.

Soon McKinney's crews begin to clear the timber and lay out streets. Homes and hotels are built, not the rugged country cabins typical of the area, but elegant homes and hotels enhanced with goods that were all brought into the area by the railroad, and sold by McKinney & Walton Mercantile, the town's first store.

From 1890 to 1900 Blue Ridge grows 400%. It has now been named the county seat.

If you were an attorney coming up by train from Atlanta to try a case in Fannin County, before 1896 you would have get off the train at Mineral Bluff and take a small horse drawn carriage known as a "hack" 3 1/2 miles to the courthouse in Morganton.

Now there's a brand new courthouse in Blue Ridge replacing the first courthouse in Morganton.

Blue Ridge, Georgia; Today.

Photo by Steve Procko

c 1910-1920
The Mineral Springs at Blue Ridge

As the 20th Century dawns you are no longer alone, but surrounded by people; residents, merchants, railroad workers, traveling salesmen, and visitors. The sidewalks are wood and in a few places marble.

Blue Ridge is booming and the railroad is the reason. Six trains a day arrive, three from Atlanta, and three from Knoxville, Tennessee. The railroad offers lots of job opportunities thanks to the locomotive repair shop located north of the depot. The men whose jobs it is to maintain the locomotives bring their families and build homes too.

Then suddenly in 1906, you shift around nervously on your comfortable log and watch as an unexpected change occurs. L&N management decides to move the large locomotive shop to Etowah, Tennessee.

Many of your new neighbors, that had arrived over the last nineteen years with the railroad pack up and move away, following their jobs to the north.

Things begin to slow down in Blue Ridge.

You sense that something has to happen for the betterment of the community. That something comes from the Reverend Joel W. Butts (1850-1920), pastor of the Blue Ridge Baptist Church, when he discovers three mineral springs just south of town. You watch intently as he cleans out the springs and then gather around him with your neighbors as he reveals that he had the water analyzed, and the springs are something special.

It is said that drinking the water benefited one's general health because the springs have magnesium, iron and sulphur.

While you and your neighbors may have questioned the worth of the water, others testified that drinking the healing waters and breathing the clean air saved their lives. "[I] arrived in Blue Ridge to find a glad welcome, a town full of smiling faces. We took walks to the mineral springs together through the cool woods and along the shady trails," said Mabel M. Richards, a nurse who came to town to restore her health.

Tourism. In 1906, it became critical to the continued existence of Blue Ridge. With it came growth.

By 1920 Blue Ridge's well-known mineral springs attracted hundreds of visitors annually. The Georgia Baptist Assembly is located nearby on two hundred acres. On another fifty-two acres is the Mary P. Willingham School for Girls. Numerous hotels and homes have also been built, many of which are spacious and elegant.

It was the mineral springs that saved the town when the railroad shops moved, establishing Blue Ridge as a tourist destination and health resort. Progress and change. In fact, the bustle of activity, sound of trains, tourists, visitors, and shopping opportunities might back then remind you of today.

"People came from South Georgia, Atlanta, places like that, mostly during July and August. Folks stayed for weeks at the hotel and boarding houses. They thought the water would heal them if they drank it and they carried it away in jugs, It smelled like swamp water to me."
- Eva Baugh

John A. Witzel's Blue Ridge Inn c.1900

The History of the Hook & Eye:
The Rugged Railroad Line Through The Mountains
By Steve Procko

The blast of the train whistle that signaled the first run of the Blue Ridge Scenic Railway resonated through the streets of Blue Ridge in 1998. But the rails it traveled on have a history going back over 160 years, with a 160-plus-mile-route that went from Marietta to Knoxville, part of which became known as the "Hook & Eye" Line. Through its long history, various parts of the line have operated under at least nine different names.

But the first 50 years is a tale full of big ideas, engineering schemes, mergers, bankruptcies and acquisitions. In a revolving door atmosphere, five different railroad presidents came and went.

It all started with the Ellijay Railroad chartered in 1854. The proposed pathway was first surveyed in 1858 by civil engineer and West Point graduate James F. Cooper (1814-1869), who had previously served from 1843-1849 as superintendent of the United States mint in Dahlonega

where a lot of wealth flowed from coins that where minted from Georgia gold.

Yet ironically, it was the lack of wealth that delayed any construction from ever starting. Then everyone's attention was suddenly diverted by the Civil War. In fact, the lack of railroad transportation through this part of the North Georgia mountains was the primary reason no significant Civil War battles took place here.

William Phillips
1st President M&NG

Prior to the war, William Phillips (1824-1908) was a lawyer living in Marietta, and the leading advocate for the Ellijay Railroad.

During the war he was the commander of "Phillips Legion" (CSA) until he was disabled by typhoid.

James F. Cooper
First Surveyor for the line known as the Ellijay Railroad.

This circa 1877-78 photograph is the only known image of the Dahlonega Mint building taken by Julius L. Straub. It was destroyed by fire in December 1878. Cooper was the mint superintendent from 1843 to 1849.

Why build a railroad from Marietta on north into the mountains?

But Phillips never forgot the dream of a railroad into the North Georgia mountains, and in 1870, he became the first president of the Marietta and North Georgia Railroad Company (M&NG).

Bonds were sold in order to pay for construction, but it was slow going when then the country entered an economic depression known as "The Panic of 1873" that would reverberate through the rest of the decade.

It took until 1874 to raise enough funds for construction of the M&NG to even begin, and funding to keep construction of the line moving would be a constant battle. But rails were finally laid in Marietta with the initial line being built in narrow gauge.

Standard gauge railroad width, like the tracks the Blue Ridge Scenic Railroad runs on today, are four feet, eight and a half inches wide. Narrow gauge rails are just three feet wide. When they began to build the line, the hope was to convert everything to standard gauge sometime in the future.

Since the southern end of the "Hook & Eye" Line was first built as a narrow gauge railway, the right-of-way that the rails were built on were narrow too, with tight curves and steep hills that fit the smaller rails. When the line was eventually upgraded to standard gauge, because of the expense of additional grading, they didn't enlarge the right-of-way, limiting the speeds the standard gauge trains could run at.

The reasons for building the railroad were more about hauling the area's rich resources than hauling the area's passengers.

It would provide cost-effective transportation for marble quarries in Tate, Georgia, logging throughout the region, and copper mining in and around Ducktown, Tennessee.

In the Copper Basin in the late 1870s, ore was being hauled by wagons 30 miles west on the Old Copper Road to meet the train at Cleveland, Tennessee. The two-day trip was time-consuming and expensive. Eventually the lack of railroad transportation to haul the ore caused the mines to fail. Without the mines as customers, it made no sense for the railroad to go there, so the planned initial route to Ducktown was cancelled. It was replaced by a new route a little to the east by way of Murphy, North Carolina.

After Murphy, the new M&NG route would follow the Hiwassee River north, then northwest to Ettowah, Tennessee. A connection there would take you all the way to Knoxville.

The additional benefits for this new route were that at Murphy passengers and freight would be able to also connect with the Western North Carolina Railroad that went to Asheville. However, construction was slow going. By 1879, the rails had only reached 24 miles north from Marietta to Canton, Georgia.

The depot at Canton, Georgia.

As the Depression of the 1870s came to an end, the M&NG was in desperate need of cash. In 1880, an entrepreneur from Cincinnati, Ohio came to the rescue. Joseph Kinsey (1828-1889), had plenty of cash on hand and provided the necessary funding for the M&NG. In doing so, Kinsey became the railroad's second president.

Joseph Kinsey
2nd President M&NG

George R. Eager
M&NG's Main contractor

All through the mountains, towns were clamoring for the railroad. The arrival of the railroad was a crossroads event; changing sleepy small towns forever, and sometimes creating towns from thin air.

Even though the trains were exponentially more efficient than horse or oxen drawn wagons, you would probably be surprised at how slow they actually traveled.

Kinsey recruited George R. Eager (1843-1907), a New Englander from Newton, Massachusetts as the main contractor. Eager would become both hero and villain in this tale.

Hero because he picked up the pace of construction and got things done. Villain because in doing so, he bankrupted the railroad.

Eager took advantage of the common practice of the time throughout the south of leasing prison labor from the state to finally get things moving northward.

The twenty-two mile stretch to Jasper was reached in 1883. Twenty more miles to Ellijay followed by December 1884.

In the 1880s, the maximum speed of trains pulling freight like marble, lumber or copper ore was just twelve miles per hour.

Passenger trains were just slightly faster at twenty miles per hour.

George Eager leased prison labor from the state of Georgia to build the railroad. Seen here are convicts working on the Western North Carolina Railroad that would connect with the MN&G in Murphy, North Carolina.

The Atlanta, Knoxville and Northern Railroad's "Little Mary", a small narrow-gauge locomotive that was the first to arrive into the area that would become Blue Ridge, Georgia in June 1886.

A leading advocate for the path of the railway through Fannin County was Mike McKinney, who just happened to own the land that would become Blue Ridge. McKinney's surveying and grading for the railway played a pivotal role in getting its path to cross through his land, instead of the then county-seat of Morganton where the courthouse was located. It was a shrewd move that forever changed Fannin County.

Finally in June 1886, the locomotive "Little Mary" pulled into the site of present-day Blue Ridge. But there wasn't anything there yet. Just survey stakes placed where town's roads and lots were going to be. The future town's plat was surveyed and drawn in 1887 by McKinney and his partner, civil engineer and superintendent of construction for the railroad C. R. "Frank" H. Walton. The two men were also business partners. The firm of McKinney and Walton, one of the first buildings in Blue Ridge, provided lucrative commissary supplies for the railroad's construction workers as well as the new residents of Blue Ridge.

Because of the never-ending need for money to continue construction, 1886 also brought the railroad's third president. Newton, Massachusetts former mayor, part owner of the Boston Herald newspaper, close personal friend of George Eager, and most important-

Mike McKinney
His vision and advocacy for the route of the railroad led to the founding of Blue Ridge in 1887.

ly, another man with a lot of cash in his pockets Royal Macintosh Pulsifer (1843-1888).

On October 24, 1887, the town was officially incorporated as Blue Ridge, Georgia. By then both McKinney and Walton had built homes for themselves - the town's first.

McKinney was also actively selling lots in town, and in doing so, he officially became Blue Ridge's very first real estate agent. At the time, the rails dead-ended in what would become the center of Blue Ridge, right near the present-day depot.

Royal M. Pulsifer
3rd President M&NG

So if the train came to a dead-end, how did the train turn around so it could return to Marietta?

The answer is that it was done with a railroad 'Wye'. Now you may be asking yourself, what's a 'Wye'?

Aside from being a great scrabble word, it's a rather smart track layout that allows locomotives and their tenders to easily turn around.

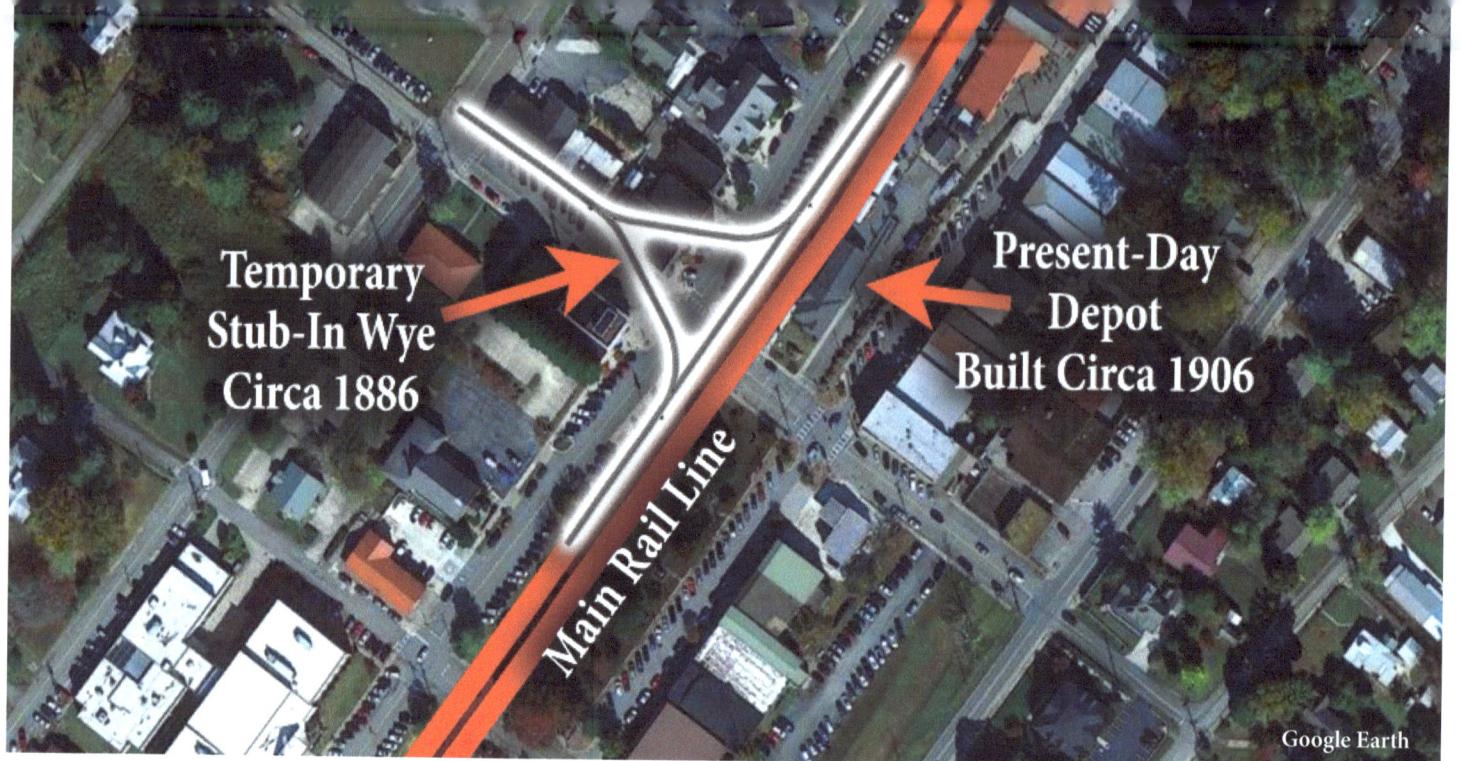

Temporary Stub-In Wye Circa 1886

Present-Day Depot Built Circa 1906

Main Rail Line

Google Earth

Blue Ridge's 'Wye' was located in the center of town for a short period of time after the railroad arrived in 1886. Since the line dead-ended at Blue Ridge, the Wye allowed for the train to turn around and return to Marietta. The Blue Ridge wye was likely there for just a few months. As railroad construction moved north, the wye was disassembled. Another Wye, known as 'Murphy Junction' still exists to this day.

The locomotive and its tender decouple from one end of the train, move around the wye, and recouple to the other end - kind of like a three-point turn for trains.

For a short time around 1886, before Blue Ridge had any buildings, it had a 'Wye' right in the middle of where the town would eventually be. When looking at where that was on Blue Ridge streets today, the tracks ran right up Depot Street towards present day city hall. Also, at that time the first depot, a smaller structure, was located across the tracks from the present one. Blue Ridge's wye was short lived, it was probably there for just a few months. As the railroad moved north of town, the wye was disassembled.

In 1887, the brick depot at Mineral Bluff, Georgia was built. Pressing northeast, the rails finally reached the outskirts of Murphy, North Carolina in Spring 1888. But things didn't go as planned. Just a half a mile from the Hiwassee river at Murphy, the owners of the last piece of

land refused to sell to the M&NG. It infamously became known as the "Roadblock at Murphy."

Passengers and cargo had to disembark the train, then take a horse drawn wagon for a last half mile to the Murphy train depot. This inconvenience would last for ten long years before the "Roadblock at Murphy" was resolved when the Hitchcock Family finally sold their land to the railroad in 1898.

But in 1888, exasperated railroad president Pulsifer had no other option but to abandon the Murphy route and revisit the original route that took the railroad line towards Ducktown, Tennessee.

The main line to Murphy, became a dead-end spur, and what had been planned as the dead end spur near Ducktown to benefit the copper mines, became the new main line.

Needless to say, this was costly.

Depot at Mineral Bluff, Georgia - circa 1900

A railroad wye that became known as "Murphy Junction" was built north of Blue Ridge. That wye allowed trains to maneuver and turn around in order to go to Ducktown, Murphy, or Blue Ridge. Part of the wye is still being used today by the Blue Ridge Scenic Railway.

The stress of all the M&NG problems must have been too much for Pulsifer, who owned most of the M&NG stock and was additionally embarrassed by a series of bad speculative investments. Royal Macintosh Pulsifer took his own life at his mansion in Newton, Massachusetts in October 1888.

Lenox Smith
4th President M&NG

The task of rerouting the line was passed on to Lenox Smith (1843-1924), a New York railroad investor and engineer, who became the M&NG's fourth president. Amidst all the chaos, Smith looked to Eager, who remained the line's chief engineer, to get things finished.

By the summer of 1889, the tracks reached the Georgia/Tennessee border at Copperhill.

On June 30, 1890, two of George Eager's crews raced each other, working at the same time, the "Knoxville Southern" crew working southbound and the M&NG crew working northbound from the Georgia Tennessee border finally converged around Apalachia, Tennessee in the Hiwassee Gorge. They celebrated by driving in the final spike.

The City of Knoxville promised a $275,000 dollar bonus if the line was completed before July 1. George Eager, who was responsible for dividing the bonus money amongst the crews, collected the winnings and promptly skipped town heading back to Massachusetts. Many unhappy Georgia and Tennessee workers subsequently sued Eager. In early 1894, a court battle took place in Knoxville, and Eager lost.

"This decree will carry joy to the hearts of many well-known Knoxville men who were almost ruined by George R. Eager and his railroad schemes," reported the *Knoxville Journal*.

With the new train line finally providing regular freight and passenger service throughout the mountains, the town of Blue Ridge grew and prospered.

But the railroad itself couldn't pay its bills. The M&NG railroad defaulted on bond interest payments in 1891 and went into receivership under the watch of Marietta's James Bolan Glover (1841-1926). Finally, the Marietta & North Georgia Railroad faced foreclosure in August 1895. Its assets were sold for 10 cents on the dollar. Lots of local folks in the small towns along the railway had been investing or had accepted payment for services in M&NG stock and bonds over the years while the railroad was built.

With foreclosure, the stocks and bonds became worthless.

Stock certificate owned by George R. Eager for 160 shares of M&NG stock.

№ 89

MARIETTA AND NORTH GEORGIA

160 SHA

Rail-Road **Company**

OF GEORGIA.

This Certifies that George R. Eager is entitled to One hundred and sixty Shares of the Capital Stock

*"Eager and Kinsey took over the work done,
and completed the line agreeing to pay in stock for the new railroad.
The few of us remaining alive today are still looking for that stock"*

- Mike McKinney reminiscing in 1923 to the losses he incurred in the construction of the railroad.

Henry K. McHarg
5th President M&NG

Blue Ridge's Mike McKinney was just one of many Georgia and Tennessee businessmen and workmen who suffered losses in the fiasco brought about by George Eager.

With foreclosure, the railroad's name changed again, becoming the Atlanta, Knoxville and Northern Railroad (AK&N) and acquired president number five - Henry K. McHarg (1851-1942), who it might be said bears a striking resemblance to the banker in a popular board game.

Meanwhile in 1901, George Eager filed for personal bankruptcy in New England owing more than 1.4 million dollars to nearly 200 creditors, most of whom were residents of Knoxville, Tennessee and Atlanta, Georgia

From 1902 to 1905, the Louisville and Nashville (L&N) railroad acquired the AK&N's stock. They would successfully run the railroad for the next 80 years. A maintenance shop located in Blue Ridge, provided jobs in the area until being relocated by the L&N to Etowah, Tennessee in 1906.

The "Hook & Eye" Line, as the route through the mountains became known, had a tremendous impact on the region's economy. The biggest commodity impacted by the railroad was logging. The logs that were hauled out of the North Georgia mountains found a market in the plywood plants and lumber mills. The copper mines of the Copper Basin also experienced a resurgence because of the ability to move resources efficiently as a result of the railroad's growth to Etowah, Tennessee. The earlier 1885 spur line for the marble quarries to the south in Tate, Georgia had the same effect.

The locomotive shop that was located at Blue Ridge, Georgia - circa 1900.

Circa 1890s - Atlanta. Knoxville and Northern Stock Certificate.

Finally, people in the mountains had an inexpensive and reliable source of transportation as passenger trains maintained daily schedules north to Knoxville and south to Atlanta.

In 1900 at Murphy, North Carolina the AK&N provided one daily round trip passenger train. Blue Ridge became the hub so that a traveler could leave first thing in the morning from Murphy and connect to another train heading either north to Knoxville or south to Atlanta at Blue Ridge. A train connection back to Murphy on the spur from Blue Ridge allowed return travel into North Carolina. With these connections, sometimes Blue Ridge saw three passenger trains at its depot at the same time. For a time, eight trains a day provided service between Atlanta and Knoxville through Blue Ridge.

In 1906, the L&N railroad completed eighty miles of new track that became known as the "New Line." This faster route to the west traveled over flatter terrain from Marietta through Cartersville and Fairmont, Georgia, then on north to Etowah, Tennessee.

The "Hook & Eye" Line obtained the additional moniker of "Old Line" as both routes were still used by the L&N railroad. On Saturday July 4, 1931, thousands took the "Old Line" to Blue Ridge from Marietta to witness the grand opening festivities of newly created Lake Toccoa, later to be renamed Blue Ridge Lake.

As the Great Depression hit the country, the number of both passenger and freight trains making the run between Atlanta and Knoxville dwindled. In 1931, there was just one daily passenger train between Atlanta and Knoxville each way on the "Hook & Eye". This meant that it as no longer possible to come to Blue Ridge from Atlanta and return in the same day.

But with the faster and more efficient "New Line," businesses began to not ship on the "Old Line" because it was so expensive, leading to the decline of use of the "Hook & Eye".

Transportation methods began evolving as cars and trucks replaced trains. There was less of a need for either passenger or freight railway service in and out of the North Georgia mountains.

This drop in supply and demand signalled change would soon be coming.

Blue Ridge, Georgia circa 1898 - Engine Number 10 of the AK&N Railroad
On the left is Fireman E. C. Howell, on the right is Engineer William F. "Bill" Garwood.
The building directly behind the locomotive is possibly Blue Ridge's first depot.

By 1940, service had been reduced to just one train a day. In 1941 the City Council of Blue Ridge would post a complaint objecting to the cancellation of train service with no result. In 1945, service was reduced further to just one "mixed train" which was basically a freight train with one passenger car at the end. Because of all of the stops to load and unload freight, it took significantly longer for passengers to arrive at their destinations.

Further complaints by the City Council of Blue Ridge in 1948 to the Georgia Railroad Commission asking to restore the service to what it once was in 1929 was rejected. In 1950 L&N supplemented its daily single train with three buses that could be taken instead. What would take the train one hour and fifteen minutes, would take the buses just 45 minutes. It was a technique used at the time to force the closure of unprofitable rail lines. It allowed the railroad to show ridership data to the Interstate Commerce Commission and prove that an area's transportation needs could easily be met with buses.

By 1951, L&N finally ended passenger service, but freight service continued though the 1980s. The Murphy, North Carolina spur route through Mineral Bluff was abandoned in 1985.

Today, the Mineral Bluff Depot is on the National Register of Historic Places and home to the Tri-State Model Railroaders who continue to work on an "HO" scale version of the L&N "Old Line".

1986 brought in the end of an era when CSX transportation petitioned the Interstate Commerce Commission to abandon the rail line from Ellijay, Georgia to the Tennessee state line.

In 1990, Wilds Pierce purchased the Georgia Northeastern Railroad, a short-line route that ran on part of the original "Hook & Eye" Line from Marietta to Ellijay. But by that time, the line from Ellijay on northward was abandoned.

Rail repairs along the abandoned line.

Volunteers clear the debris off the tracks.

The Georgia Department of Transportation (GDOT) stepped in and took over the ownership of the rail line's right-of-way and soon the rugged mountain landscape began reclaiming the rail's pathway. Vegetation and saplings sprouted in the center of the tracks along with the ever-present kudzu blanket of greenery.

It was as if the earth was taking back the rails. They would soon be no more.

In the town of Blue Ridge, several civic-minded folks recognized that a valuable transportation resource was in danger of being lost. They formed The Blue Ridge Mountain Preservation Society and approached Georgia Northeastern's Wilds Pierce asking if he could help establish a scenic railroad with the goal of stimulating the area's economy. By that time, nothing had run over the tracks near Blue Ridge for years.

Dead tree trunks, weeds, kudzu, crossties, and damaged rails had to be removed. It was back breaking work, accomplished by volunteers. The largest and most effective volunteer group was the National Association of Railroad Car Owners. Members of this group own railroad cars, which are small rail-riding vehicles used commercially for rail repair. These enthusiasts could take their personally owned vehicles where a locomotive could not go. Railcars are smaller and lighter and could move on somewhat damaged tracks.

"It was a mess, between Blue Ridge and McCaysville no train had run for six years. On the Ellijay side the tracks had not been used for twenty years. We had to remove 12,000 crossties," said volunteer Carl Hymen. "A bunch of us spent all our spare time clearing for a year and a half. Cutting brush became the thing to do."

With the help of all those volunteers, operations on the Blue Ridge Scenic Railway began in May 1998. The influx of people coming into Fannin County and the Copper Basin became the spark that fuels the tourist economy of today.

Riding the Blue Ridge Scenic Railway is nostalgic,
and the beauty of the mountains,
as viewed when seated in a moving train car,
is more popular than ever before.

Watch a YouTube video about the 'Hook & Eye' line.

Photo by Steve Procko

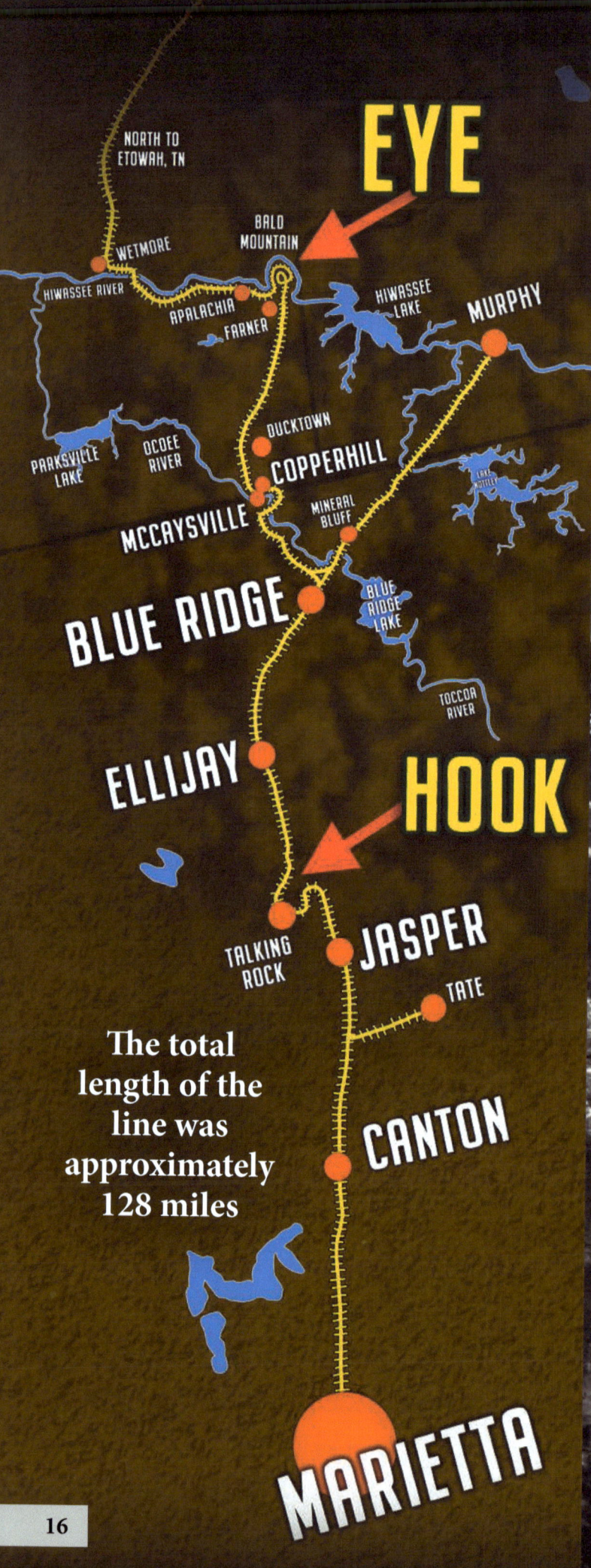

EYE

NORTH TO
ETOWAH, TN

BALD
MOUNTAIN

WETMORE

HIWASSEE RIVER

APALACHIA

FARNER

HIWASSEE
LAKE

MURPHY

DUCKTOWN

PARKSVILLE
LAKE

OCOEE
RIVER

COPPERHILL

LAKE
NOTTELY

MINERAL
BLUFF

MCCAYSVILLE

BLUE RIDGE

BLUE
RIDGE
LAKE

TOCCOA
RIVER

ELLIJAY

HOOK

TALKING
ROCK

JASPER

TATE

The total
length of the
line was
approximately
128 miles

CANTON

MARIETTA

The Hook & Eye Line gets its name from the two unique pieces of railroad engineering that were required to create the route through the rugged mountains.

The railroad line would take more than twenty-five years to complete.

The main reasons?

The incredibly difficult mountain terrain, constantly changing management, lack of money and a bankruptcy.

The Hook

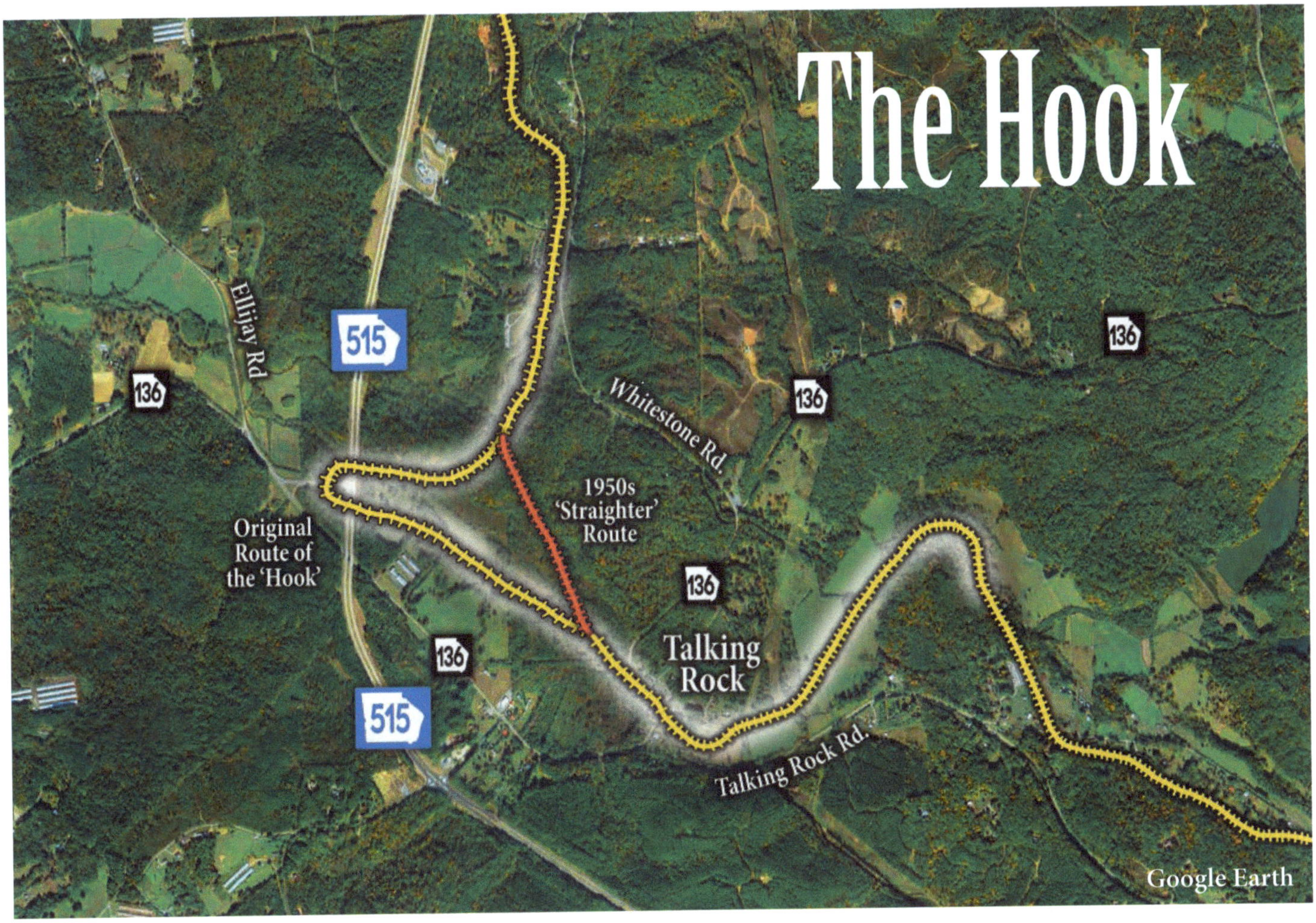

The map labels visible on the satellite image:

Ellijay Rd

515

136

136

136

136

136

515

Whitestone Rd.

1950s 'Straighter' Route

Original Route of the 'Hook'

Talking Rock

Talking Rock Rd.

Google Earth

The nickname **"Hook and Eye Line"** came from two distinct features of rail design engineered to traverse the rough mountain terrain.

"The Hook" referred to a double reverse curve in the the rail line near the town of Talking Rock, between Jasper and Ellijay, Georgia. There were two switch back horseshoe bends designed to manage the steep ascent or descent at Tate Mountain.

When viewed from above, it looked like the rail line had a hook in it. But the end result slowed the trains down, so the hook was straightened in the 1950s. The location of the western part of the hook was buried under Georgia Highway 515 when it was built.

Talking Rock, Georgia today, site of the 'Hook'.

Photo by Steve Procko

17

The Crazy Route of 'The Old W'

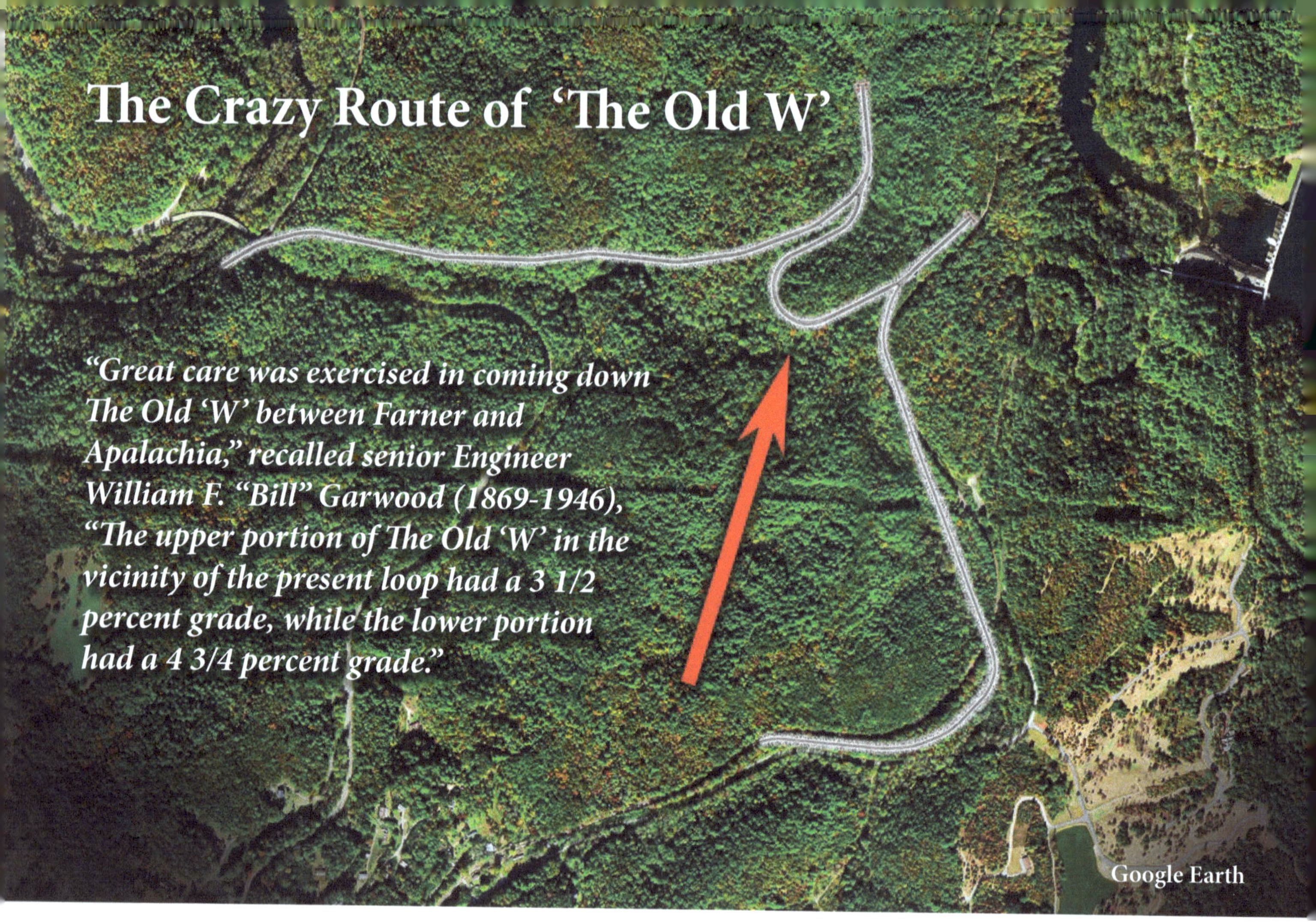

"Great care was exercised in coming down The Old 'W' between Farner and Apalachia," recalled senior Engineer William F. "Bill" Garwood (1869-1946), *"The upper portion of The Old 'W' in the vicinity of the present loop had a 3 1/2 percent grade, while the lower portion had a 4 3/4 percent grade."*

Google Earth

"The Eye" is an amazing feet of engineering ingenuity built in 1898, designed to deal with the steep mountain grade.

In 1890, near Farner, Tennessee when George Eager rushed to complete the line, he encountered a small problem near Bald Mountain where the terrain dropped some 200 feet down to the Hiwassee River. The terrain was so steep that a double switchback was built. It formed the shape of an inverted "W". (Note: It might also be said that an inverted "W" is actually just the letter "M", but back then it was warmly known as "The Old W").

The distinctive double switchback in the line required locomotives to stop and then back up for a ways and then move forward. They could only take a couple of cars at a time through the switchback, making the process painfully slow. It soon became clear that the double switchback was untenable. A better idea of how to traverse the treacherous drop in grade needed to be found.

Thomas A. Aber designed 'The Eye'. It was built in 1898.

Blue Ridge, Georgia; July 4, 1931.
Visitors arriving from Atlanta to celebrate the grand opening of new "Lake Toccoa".

The solution was devised by Louisiana-born Thomas A. Aber (1860-1924), a civil engineer on loan to the AK&N from the L&N railroad. Aber designed a new route where the rail line would have made two complete loops around Bald Mountain. When Aber finally showed it to railroad president Henry McHarg, McHarg tallied up the costs of such an enormous undertaking, then ordered the design be simplified to just one loop.

Riding the rails was an exciting, modern thing to do, and Blue Ridge became a tourist destination in the early 1900s. But there was just a slight problem: the mountainous terrain was not built for speed and was extremely expensive to operate.

In fact, the highest elevation point on the entire line between Atlanta and Knoxville is at Blue Ridge, Georgia, right in front of the old 1930s-era courthouse, which is currently home to the Blue Ridge Mountains Arts Association. Steam engines pulling too many cars would spin their wheels when they reached this point, and would have to decouple some of their cars to make it into Blue Ridge.

The depot at Blue Ridge, Georgia as passenger train service came to an end.

19

The Eye

The Garwood Brothers: Railroad pioneers of the 'Hook & Eye' Line.

Bill Garwood (left) and his brother Sid (right) witnessed the earliest days the 'Hook & Eye' line.

In May 1882, 13-year-old Bill Garwood (1869-1946) was walking to school in Canton, Georgia with his older brother. Their path crossed over the tracks of the new M&NG, which was under construction. Bill kicked the shiny new rails and excitedly said, "Let's get a job on the railroad."

They walked up to the construction foreman who laughed at the two boys and asked what they could possibly do on the railroad? "Anything you tell me to do," Bill replied.

Bill was just eighteen when in June 1886 he brought the small, narrow-gauge locomotive named "Little Mary" into the empty field that would quickly grow into the town of Blue Ridge. The locomotive was tiny, with just four wheels, and its 'passenger' car was was a jury-rigged old boxcar with seats and oil lamps mounted to its sidewalls and a big old pot-bellied stove in its center to provide warmth. Younger brother Sid (1871-1957) began working for the M&NG in August 1886.

The Garwood brothers both worked for the various railroads that ran through Blue Ridge all the way into the L&N days and the 1940s. Combined between them, they had a total of more than 120 years of service.

October 1940 L&N Railroad employee magazine cover shows a brave crew member perilously running on top of a boxcar as his train approaches the bridge to enter 'The Eye'.

'The Eye' is some 8,000 feet in length. It rises 426 feet in less than six miles, with a grade of less than 1.5%, which means there is a less than a 1.5 foot vertical rise for each 100 feet in track.
That final design of the distinctive loop can seen in aerial photographs taken in the 1940s.
Depending on the length of the train, it was possible for the engineer in the locomotive to pass over the bridge and see the back of his own train.
This route around Bald Mountain is still in use today and is known as 'The Hiwassee Loop.'

The point where the tracks of 'The Eye' cross over themselves.

Photo by Steve Procko

Photo by Steve Procko

Georgia and Tennessee's Quirky State Line

By Kathy Thompson

Twelve miles to the north of Blue Ridge is the Great Copper Basin. The term recalls the mining history of the adjacent communities of McCaysville, Georgia, and Copperhill, Tennessee. Hugging both sides of the river that flows out of Blue Ridge Lake, it is not always clear in which town you are standing or visiting. As tourism developed, multiple bright blue dotted lines were painted designating significant division points between the two towns.

Tourists line up at the corner of Toccoa Avenue and Highway 5 to have their photo taken with one foot in Georgia and the other in Tennessee. While all of this involves lots of laughter, there are fascinating and occasionally serious consequences derived from a state line that zigzags in and out of properties. A good place to explore both towns and the state-line is where passengers depart from the Blue Ridge Scenic Railway excursion.

When the train arrives in Copperhill and McCaysville from

Blue Ridge, it parks in two states. With an engine at each end, one is in Georgia and the other Tennessee. The string of train cars between the locomotives are also split between the states. When passengers are ready to depart, the conductor proudly explains the state line situation. Surprised passengers are instructed to depart from the two

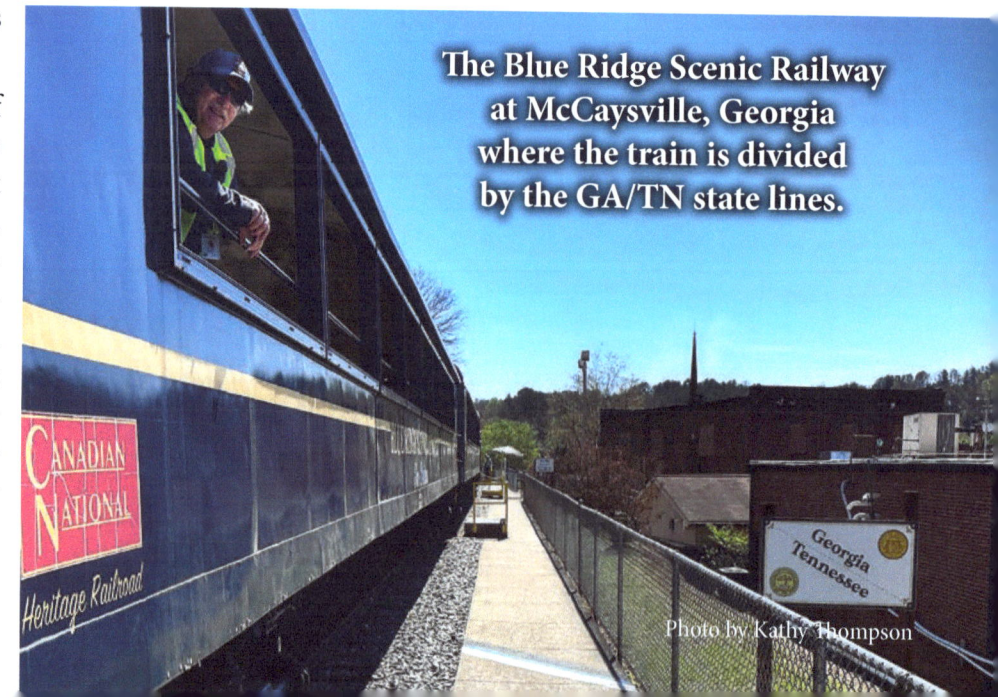

The Blue Ridge Scenic Railway at McCaysville, Georgia where the train is divided by the GA/TN state lines.

Photo by Kathy Thompson

ends of the train depending on their car location.

Half step down in Georgia and half in Tennessee.

A Church and a Grocery Store

2 As you step off the train and begin walking down Toccoa Avenue, on the hill behind the train is the Catholic Church, which is split in half at an angle by the state line. The altar is located in Georgia while seating for

Shopping or Dining in Two States at the Same Location

Between Highway 5 and Bridge Street, along Toccoa Avenue, there are five buildings containing eating and shopping establishments. Rum Cake Lady, the building closest to Highway 5, is wholly in Georgia.

The other four buildings are bisected at an angle by the state line with interesting results. Technically all

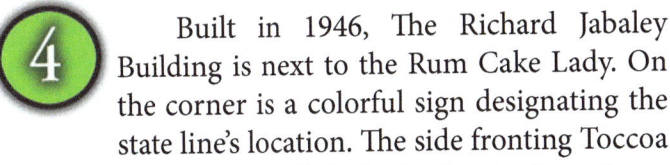

the congregants lies in Tennessee. One can take communion in Georgia and attend mass in pews located in Tennessee. Weddings are equally interesting.

Vows are said in Georgia in front of guests setting in Tennessee. When the couple leaves, walking proudly down the aisle to the strains of Mendelssohn, they will cross the state line.

3 Back down the hill on Toccoa Avenue, there's a supermarket that's been here for years.

The state line bisects its parking lot, then goes through the back corner of the building leaving the entire shopping area in Georgia. As you push your cart of bagged groceries to your car, you go from one state to the other. Some cars in the adjacent lot are parking in Tennessee and others in Georgia.

four pay taxes in Tennessee. Still, the state line is acknowledged by both states to divide each property.

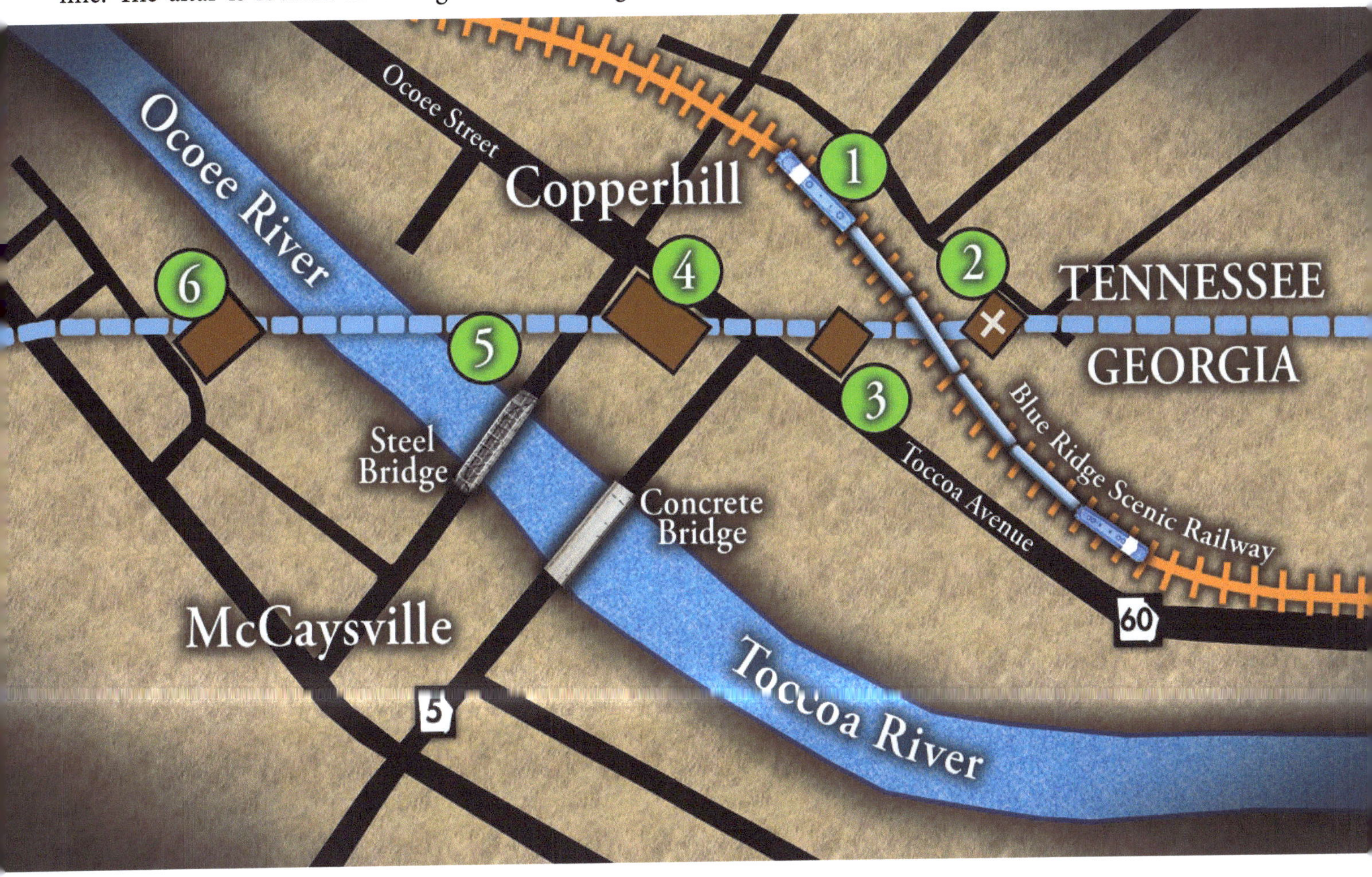

4 Built in 1946, The Richard Jabaley Building is next to the Rum Cake Lady. On the corner is a colorful sign designating the state line's location. The side fronting Toccoa Avenue is in Tennessee while the back is in Georgia.

For decades Richard Jabaley (1904-1981) and sons ran a dry goods store that operated until 1990 and the building was rented to a furniture store. If you bought a couch there, you would be told that if they delivered it via the back door you would pay Georgia sales taxes or Tennessee sales taxes through the front. The choice depended on which was lower!

Perhaps this was just a joke but with the doors in differing states, it might just might be true.

23

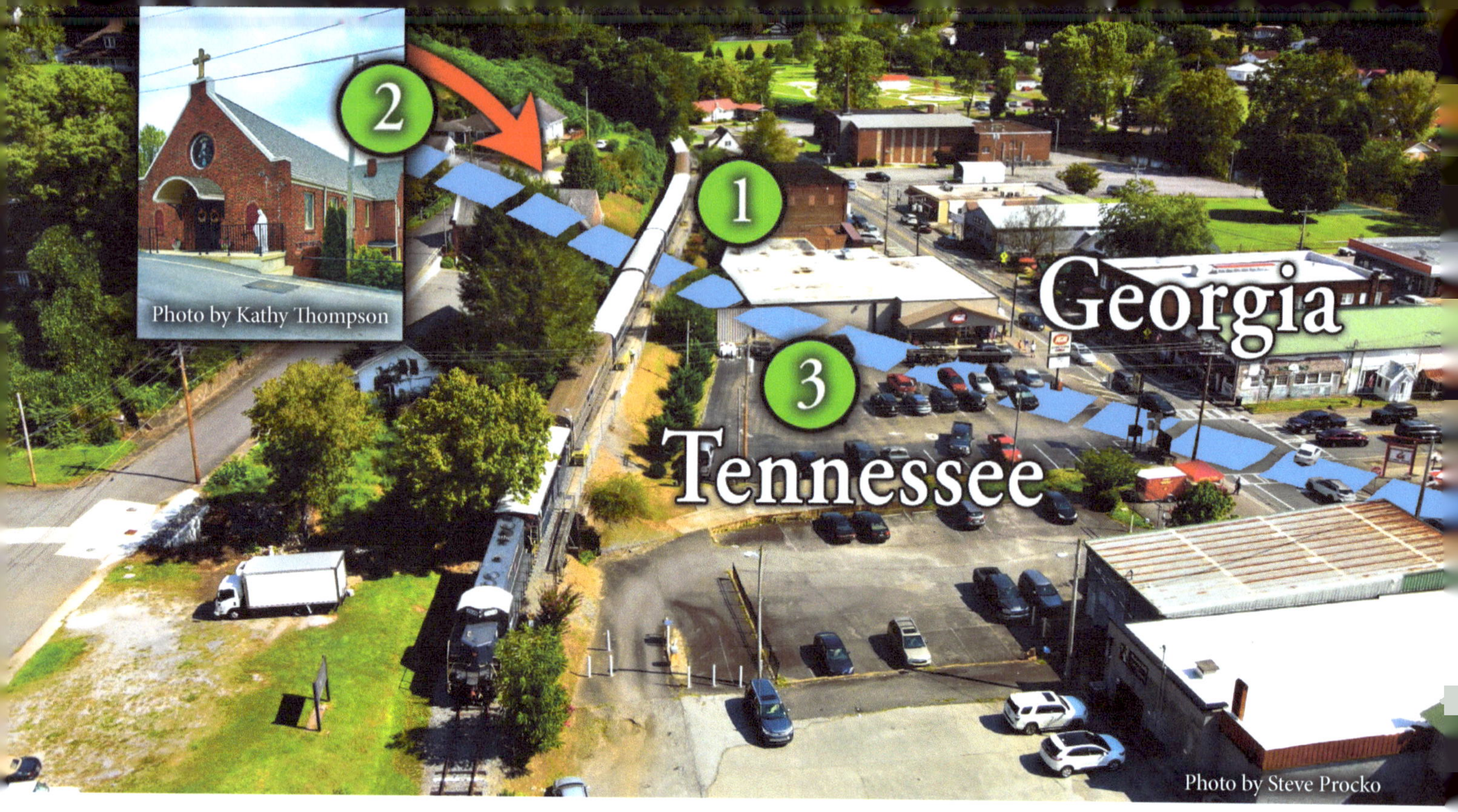

Photo by Kathy Thompson

Georgia

①

②

③

Tennessee

Photo by Steve Procko

The next two businesses are eateries in which the dining areas are in Tennessee and the back of the establishments in Georgia. As a result, one can eat in Tennessee, food that was cooked in Georgia. If you leave your table to use the restrooms, you are crossing the state line. While all pay in Tennessee, you could be eating in Georgia if you are sitting at a back table. Remember to claim residency in a state, you need to live in that state more than half the year, so choose the table you eat at carefully.

You can see where the blue line is marked in the shop at the back of the Maloof Building which was built in 1921 by Syrian immigrant Nassir Ackel "Louis" Maloof (1895-1994). For seven decades, he and later his family ran a successful dry goods business. Today it has been subdivided, but still involves retail sales.

The State Line in the Copper Basin 1910 vs 1941 in Copperhill/McCaysville

When you are standing on that painted blue line at the corner of the old Richard Jabaley building, look down and you will find a round bronze marker embedded in the sidewalk. "That is what really counts," says local surveyor Lane Bishop, "markers make it hard to manipulate or change property lines." When a state line is surveyed and set or reset, the surveyor places markers along the state line's path. So this marker would have been officially installed by the legal authority of both states.

Over the years the sidewalks have been raised, but the marker itself never moved, remaining firmly in place where it was originally installed. Today, there is a circular dirt-filled hole more than six inches deep where the marker is buried.

In the past, survey markers could be trees, a gravestone, business or other landmarks. The brass marker system was intended to provide a more lasting reference. Today surveys, are accomplished using GPS systems.

④

Stores and restaurants in Copperhill some bisected by the state line.

An official survey crew from the Georgia Department of Transportation (GDOT) placed the bronze marker in 1941. Called a Geodetic Control Station, it is officially listed in a GDOT registry with the following technical information:

S.L.10 (Fannin Co. 1941) Station is on present Georgia-Tennessee State line where Georgia Route #5 crosses in Copperhill. The mark is a bronze disk set in concrete sidewalk and stamped, "Georgia Highway Board, S.L.10, Dec. 1941." The mark is just east of base of Pure Oil Sign near Pure Oil Service Station on corner r: on west side of road across from Dickey's Motor Company; the service station is at "T" intersection. Grid zenith to Gd. Good. Station 35A-40 which is 811.1 feet from station is 304° 31' 15".

		Coordinates
Latitude	- 34° 59' 17.00"	x - 439.036.0
Longitude	- 84° 22' 12.75"	y - 1,814,630.4

Photos by Kathy Thompson

It is said that in 1941 when finishing this section of the state line the survey crew spent an evening in a local bar getting skunk drunk. The next morning they were well hungover when they set the line through McCaysville/Copperhill. Another version has the crew getting drunk on moonshine just north of the town and then refusing to come back and finish. No matter what version it always involves drinking and a skewed state line. As a result, a number of locals doubt the accuracy of the line.

The sign placed by the Merchant's association stands at the corner of the old Jabaley store building. It sits about 10 inches from the bronze marker. This choice of location is practical considering the sign would block the sidewalk if it was by the marker. So technically, when you pose for a photo with the sign behind you, the line is really 10 inches to your left.

1818 State Line Survey was OFF the Mark

The northwest section of the Georgia/Tennessee state line was problematic from its inception. As a result of initial mistakes in 1818, disputes between the two states have arisen regularly. Starting in 1887, the Georgia legislature challenged the currently accepted boundary. Legal challenges have been lodged in 1905, 1915, 1922, 1941, 1947, 1971, 2008, 2012 and continue to this day. While all previous attempts to change the border have been unsuccessful, such a change would move the town of Copperhill into Georgia. This can be a very unsettling possibility for those who live in the Copper Basin. "I'm a Tennessean and I bought a house in Copperhill," a homeowner in Copperhill announced with conviction.

When Congress voted to make Tennessee a state in 1796, the 35th north parallel was set as the state's southern border. At that time the line was in indigenous Cherokee lands. It was not until 1818 that Georgia and Tennessee chose to map their common border.

First mathematicians had to calculate the 35th north parallel, then surveyors went east and marked the boundary. They had to determine the point in the western corner of Georgia where Georgia begins and Tennessee ends.

It was the mathematicians, and their lack of proper equipment, that started the trouble. James Camak (1795-1847), a professor at the University of Georgia was paired with James S. Gaines (1794-1879) from Tennessee.

The potential for disaster was high. Locating a parallel with a nautical sextant is less than exact. Camak was aware of the instrument's limitations and requested better equipment from the Georgia Governor. Not wanting to pay the costs of modern 1818 surveying equipment, Governor William Rabun (1771-1819) refused, and Camak had to make do.

To add to the near certainty of a mistake, the charts used to calculate the border were flawed. Readings taken on the sextant were then interpreted with tables called "ephemerides." Camak himself expressed concern, "[They] were not such as I could have wished them to be." The combination of problems resulted in an inaccurate location, one that the survey crew used to draw the state line.

A nifty song you can dance to while straddling the geographic phenomenon known as the Georgia-Tennessee state line:

The State Line Hop

Put your right foot in Georgia...
Your left in Tennessee...
Now hop up and down,
For your friends to see.

A Geo-Phenom - not to be topped...
That's what's called the State-Line Hop.

Hopping like a spring...
Spin half way around...
Your feet flipped states,
As you land on the ground.

You're amazed - as places are swapped...
It's the funky dance called the State-Line Hop.

Hoppin' up and down...
in Copperhill...
Then all of a sudden
Mc-Cays-ville.

A Geo-Phenom not to be topped...
Everyone's doin' the State-Line Hop.

Your friends are impressed...
And quickly join in...
All hoppin' up and down,
flippin' states they've been.

A Geo-Phenom not to be topped...
It's a crazy dance called the State-Line Hop.

Next time 'round
Wave your hands in the air...
Then spin round again,
Adding personal flair.

Passin' time at the whistle stop...
Where everyone's doin' the State-Line Hop.

A blue dashed line
Divides two states...
Your bouncing' up and down,
And the feeling is great.

A Geo-Phenom not to be topped...
Everyone's doing the State-Line Hop.
Everyone's doing the State-Line Hop.
Everyone's doing the State-Line Hop.

Standing in two states at the same time.

At the point the two mathematicians determined a stone was set. Today it is referred to as the "Camak Stone." In fact the stone was placed about one mile south of the 35th north parallel compounding the problems. The survey party also flawed the lines making the line about a half mile off.

Even Camak felt the stone was not accurately set. Eight years later, after new charts were available, he attempted to run the line again. To his dismay the original calculation placed the line one mile south of the true 35th parallel in several places. He determined the northwest corner of Georgia was wrong. The "Camak Stone" was then moved north to its current, and still inaccurate location.

Will The State Line Ever Change?

Despite ten attempts by Georgia to reset the GA/TN line, the border remains the same. Legal border expert Louis DeVorsey explains, "The decisive factor is not where the surveyors meant to draw the line – it's where people have accepted the line to be over time. It's where people adjusted their lives to."

How Do I Know in Which State I Live?

One would assume the issue is decided entirely on where the state line is determined to be located. But the reality is more convoluted. Those whose homes and properties are bisected by the state line were often given permission to choose in what state they wanted to reside. For example Marion "Cap" Hamby (1877-1958), who served as Mayor of both McCaysville, Georgia and Copperhill, Tennessee, was allowed to choose more than once, without changing his residence or any alterations in the GA/TN line.

The surprise is that property owners adjacent to state lines were also allowed to choose, on which side of the state line they were on. In these cases which state one pays taxes to trumps state line maps.

Studying tax maps from both Polk County, Tennessee and Fannin County, Georgia reveal about two dozen homes that are paying taxes today based on choice, not which side of state border they live.

On one side of the river, the state line runs through properties on the streets above the grovery store. There about a dozen home owners that pay taxes in Tennessee but whose properties are to the southeast or Georgia side of the state line. This is quite legal. Those living in these properties are Tennessee residents by where they pay taxes. They legally vote in Tennessee and in a few cases have and do hold elected positions in Polk County. Another group of houses in the same situation are between West Tennessee Street and Market Street in McCaysville. Even though the state line puts them in Georgia, they are considered residents of and pay taxes to Tennessee.

Tax rules are different for businesses. The owners of the grocery store pay taxes in two states. Because the line bisects the parking lot and store storage area on the Copperhill side, they pay property taxes to Fannin County, Polk County, McCaysville, and Copperhill. All told, they pay a total of six different tax bills. Wow!

A River with Two Names

The historic steel bridge marks the point where the Toccoa River becomes the Ocoee River. The ducks and summer folks floating in tubes and canoes pay no attention to the state line or name change as they float under the bridge.

Toccoa is derived from the indigenous Cherokee *"Ta Gura Hi,"* Meaning "home of the Catawba." The Catawba were a separate tribe from the Cherokee and lived for a short time in the 1700s in this area.

Ocoee was in Cherokee *"U-wa-go-hi,"* The English version was Ocoee. It means apricot place or home of the Maypop. In the mountains of Georgia, Tennessee and North Carolina, an "old field apricot" is what the botanists call *"Passiflora incarnata"*, the native perennial wild passion flower vine that grows in abandoned fields and along the roadsides. After its lemon-sized fruit begins to yellow and wrinkle just a bit, the thin skin is easily opened so that the delicious fruit can be eaten on the spot or made into a drink, in the style of the indigenous people. The leaves and other parts can also be made into an effective sedative tea. Its Cherokee name is *"U-wa-ga,"* and some people call it a "Maypop" in English.

Mayor In Two Cities

While standing on the steel bridge, looking downstream a few hundred feet towards the southwest shore is the property once owned by Mayor Cap Hamby.

From 1923 to 1925, Hamby was Mayor of McCaysville. Then in 1937 he became Mayor of Copperhill until 1938. The state line bisected his home, with his kitchen in Georgia and his bedrooms in Tennessee.

During the interim, Cap had changed where he

McCaysville/Copperhill's steel bridge was renovated in 2024 with a new wood deck

Photo by Kathy Thompson

paid taxes from Georgia to Tennessee. Where you are taxed determines your legal residence. This unique feat earned him recognition in the Ripley's Believe It or Not newspaper feature.

Cap Hamby was the "Rigger Foreman" at the Tennessee Copper Company. He held the position for three decades and was still working at age 74. Cap was known for his booming voice, an occupational requirement for Riggers.

As a foreman, he would shout out a cadence for men heaving on lines to raise steel beams to high places or working on girders far above the ground. A hard worker at the plant and as Mayor, Cap Hamby was well respected in two states.

Changing states without moving was not uncommon at that time. Local resident Sarah Quintrell Finch (1941-2022) recalled that her family did this a couple of times. "Our reason was because of which schools our parents wanted us to attend."

It is rumored that a local business owner, who shall remain nameless, paid to neither state. He simply told each state that he was paying taxes in the other state.

The Not So Simple State Line

A ramble up and down the Tennessee/Georgia state line can sometimes be confusing. After all, it is probably important to know in which state you live. But when in doubt, choose!

McCaysville and Copperhill's Magical Mystery Steel Bridges

By Steve Procko

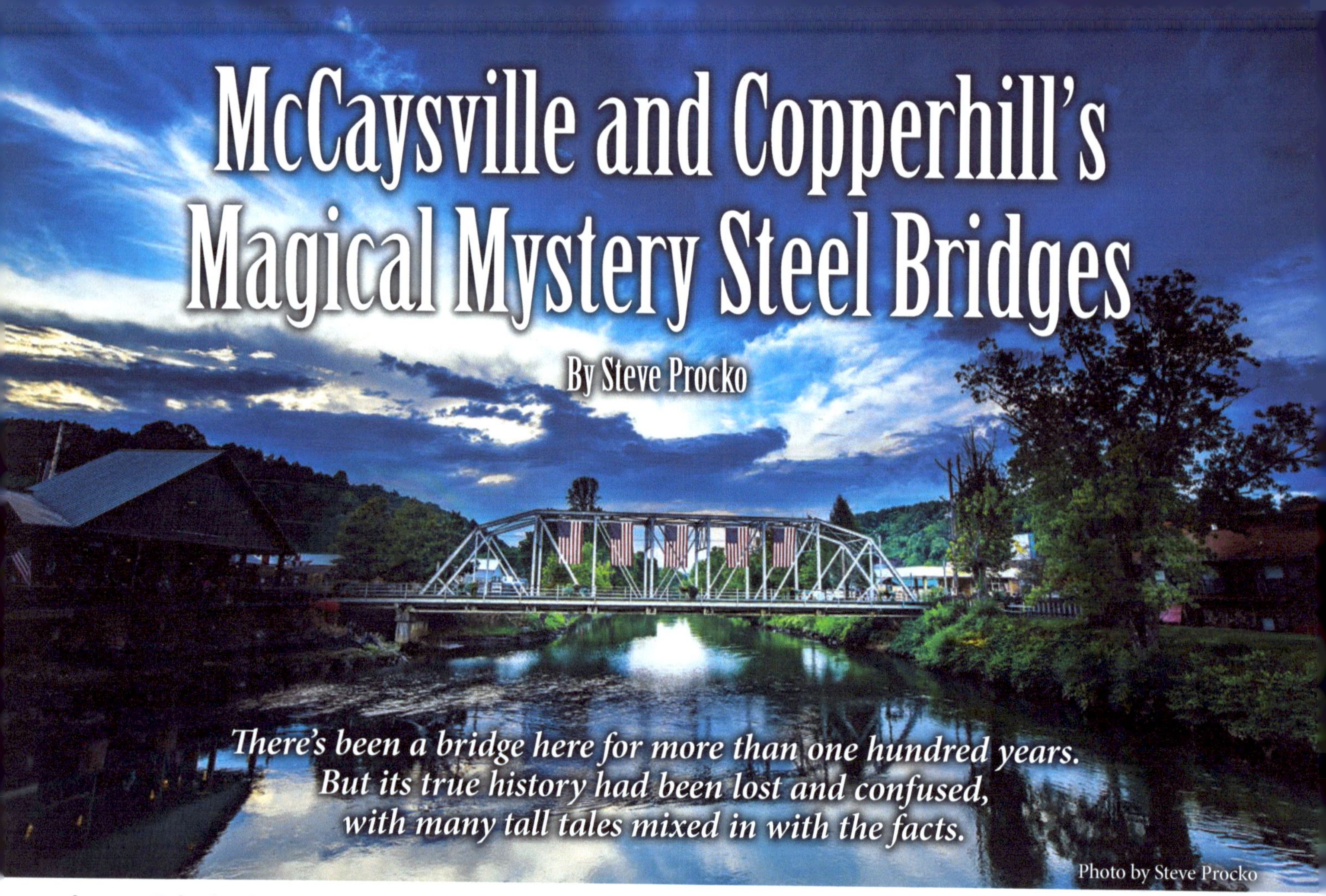

There's been a bridge here for more than one hundred years.
But its true history had been lost and confused,
with many tall tales mixed in with the facts.

Photo by Steve Procko

The bridges at McCaysville and Copperhill are part of what makes them twin-sister towns. The present-day steel bridge is actually the second steel bridge crossing the river at the same place. But it was originally built someplace else, and moved to its present location 15 years later!

There were several fords used over the Toccoa River near McCaysville and Copperhill dating back to indigenous people. A busy ferry had been working the site for decades. In 1903, a pedestrian footbridge was built to allow quicker access to either side of the Toccoa without having to wait for the ferry.

Circa 1903-1910 - Located where today's steel bridge is, a ferry crosses the Toccoa River from Copperhill to McCaysville. along with the elevated footbridge seen to the left.

The need for a better solution was apparent from the moment the footbridge was built, but it would take several years before the first steel bridge would be constructed requiring the cooperation of two states. Determining the exact dates the first steel bridge was built took some detective work, and produced conflicting results. Because around 1900, records were sparse.

The breakthrough came when looking at the details of the great fire of 1910. On two successive nights, Friday and Saturday, December 2 and 3, 1910, two fires almost completely obliterated Copperhill. Ninety-seven buildings, mostly built of pine were burned. In addition, the pedestrian footbridge partially burned, collapsing into the Toccoa.

"Survey Report for Historic Highway Bridges" (TN Survey Report) stating it was built by the Converse Bridge Company of Chattanooga, Tennessee. Finally, Robert E. Barclay places the bridge construction as 1911 in his 1975 book *"The Copper Basin 1890 to 1963."*

How can all three sources be correct? - that the bridge was built in 1909, 1910 and 1911? Well, it's because in each of those years, something significant did happen that resulted in the first steel bridge. This was before GDOT and TDOT existed. Funding to build the early roads and bridges came from the counties and the citizens and businesses living in the counties the transportation project would benefit.

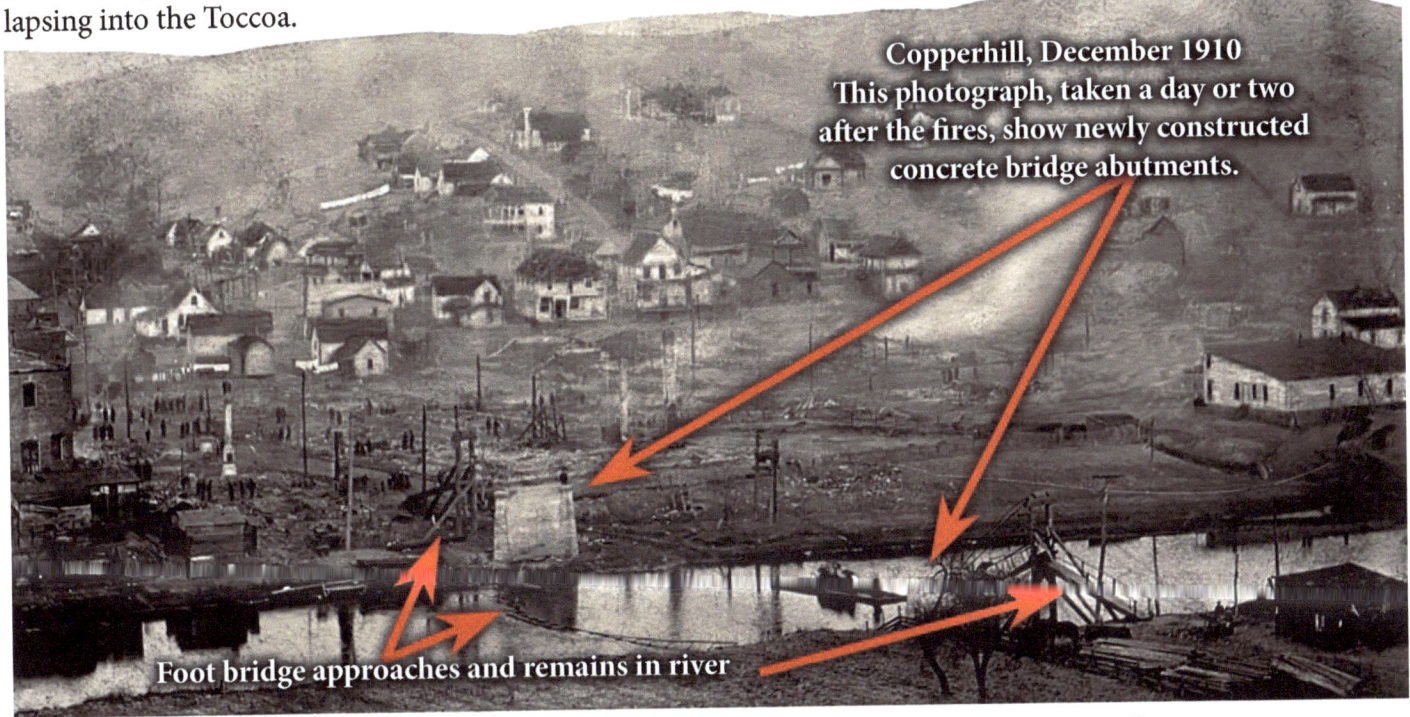

Copperhill, December 1910
This photograph, taken a day or two after the fires, show newly constructed concrete bridge abutments.

Foot bridge approaches and remains in river

A day or so after the fires, a photograph was made from the McCaysville side of the river looking back at the remains of Copperhill. In the photograph are two concrete abutments. These abutments matched later photographs of the new steel bridge, proving construction was underway in December 1910. The photograph is also a significant clue as to where the ferry and footbridge were in relationship to the first steel bridge:

They were in the same place!

The First Steel Bridge

Further pinpointing the dates of the events involved for the first steel bridge, in a 1913 political handbill for Fannin County Ordinary and Blue Ridge's former mayor Albert S. Hall (1867-1913), the bridge's construction dates were recorded as 1909-1910. 1909 was given as the published date of construction in The Tennessee Department of Transportation's

The *TN Survey Report* states "County governments, through their county courts, or less often through their quarterly courts, gradually became the most dominant force in road and bridge construction until the creation of the Tennessee State Highway Department in 1915." Each county's quarterly or county court minutes contain details of these activities.

These details reveal that counties typically funded the projects through general revenue that was sometimes supplemented with a one to fifteen cent per $100 bridge tax levied on its citizens. Frequently, the county court approved the construction of a certain bridge but deferred its erection until funds became available.

It also took the efforts of local citizens lobbying to move the projects forward. In the case of the first steel bridge, businessman Luther H. Abernathy (1886-1949) and attorney, and first mayor of Copperhill Jeff A. Hedden (1876-1922) were instrumental in getting the bridge built.

Luther H. Abernathy

A group of friends pose in front of the newly completed bridge in a "1912 Runabout Co. Liberty automobile". The man second from the left is likely Abernathy.

Abernathy and Hedden cobbled together a plan that secured the roughy $4,000 cost of construction that was split between Fannin County, Polk County and the citizens of Copperhill.

The TN Survey Report goes on to say, "Unlike most other counties, Polk County had no bridges spanning its three major rivers by the turn of the century [1900]." Feeling that ferry service hindered the county's growth, Polk County initiated an ambitious bridge building program. In 1899 the state legislature authorized the county to issue bonds for $25,000 to build bridges. However, it was not until about 1905 that the county contracted for major bridges.

At that time the county contracted the Converse Bridge Company "for $40,000 to build six bridges… [and] over the following years, the county built these six bridges and others, one at a time, primarily between 1908 and 1915."

With the money secured and the details put in place by Abernathy and Hedden, it's likely the timing of the first steel bridge was approved to be constructed around 1909.

Then construction started sometime in 1910, with the concrete abutments clearly finished at the time of the big fire. The first steel bridge was completed in 1911, probably as quickly as they could since the fire had knocked out the footbridge and the only way across the river was by ferry.

The completion of the first steel bridge was a significant milestone in the history of McCaysville and Copperhill. It set the stage for future growth and showed the value of investing in important transportation infrastructure. From 1911 onward, crossing the Toccoa River by means of a ferry or footbridge became just a memory.

Shortly after its construction, this view is from the Georgia side of the bridge looking towards Copperhill.

Vintage postcard of first steel bridge from Copperhill looking back towards McCaysville.

The specific details of the first steel bridge are well known, thanks to a 1935 survey conducted by GDOT, before the first steel bridge was raised and replaced with the current steel bridge. The survey measured the first steel bridge in detail and showed its placement across the river.

The first steel bridge was 259.6 feet long including wooden approach ramps and a wooden sidewalk on the northeast side. The floor decking was also wooden. The bridge was almost four feet higher than the current steel bridge. The approach ramps were short, eight feet long and quickly rising the four feet to the bridge deck. That's a 26.6 degree rise in just eight feet. Driving up them would have disrupted your view of the road bed, and whether or not there was another vehicle coming from the opposite direction, until you reached the bridge level. The first bridge was also more narrow, only around twelve feet wide, and would have been considered a one-lane bridge.

Can you imagine reaching the bridge level and discovering another car approaching from the opposite direction and then having to put your Model T in reverse and back down the steep ramp to allow the other car to pass?

What is perplexing is that the current steel bridge is on "Bridge Street", and one block to the southwest is a street called "Ferry Street". From the photographic evidence, the ferry and the footbridge were located on "Bridge Street", at the same place as the first steel bridge. Which leaves the reason for the name of "Ferry Street" unexplained.

1935 survey of the first (1911) steel bridge just before its replacement.

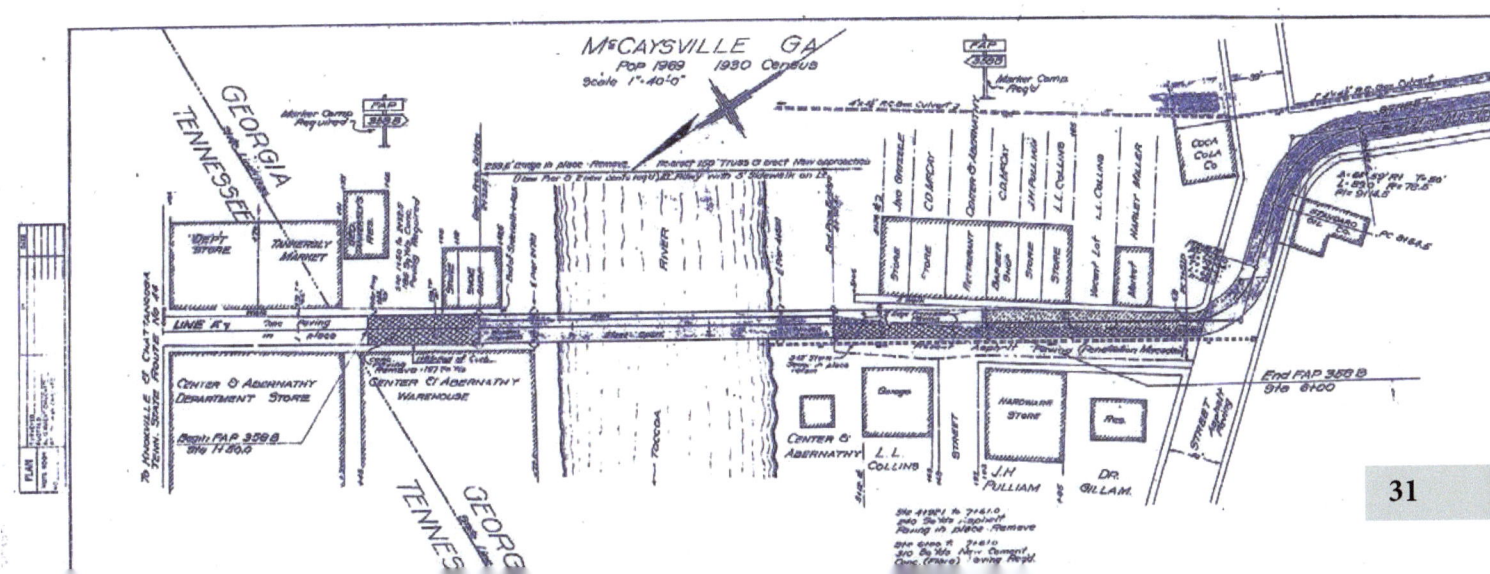

A Magical Mystery Bridge Tale

There are a couple of bridges silently spanning the Toccoa River at McCaysville, one is made of concrete and the other is made of steel. The steel bridge is the older of the two whose history has often been confused. It might be said that McCaysville's current steel bridge is a magical, mystery bridge.

The mystery is a story that claims this bridge was floated intact to McCaysville from another site up river. "He was sitting on his back porch along the river and saw it float on by," claimed one witness.

A more magical tale claims a remarkably similar-looking bridge is currently sitting below 125 feet of water under Blue Ridge Lake - with the teller of that tale claiming that he knows it as a fact!

Well, the true detective story, with all the actual facts starts back in 1916. Because in that year, President Woodrow Wilson signed into law the Federal Aid Road Act to provide funds to build roads all across the country.

In 1919, the State Highway Board, the precursor to today's GDOT was formed in Georgia to help secure those federal aid dollars. Blueprints were drawn and Fannin County was tasked with providing an estimate for construction.

On April 22, 1920, Fannin County ordinary George A. Curtis (1878-1955) filed a request for sealed bids in the "Manufacturers Record", a weekly national publication devoted to "upbuilding the nation", calling for construction of a 200 foot bridge made of 7,106 pounds of reinforcing steel over the Toccoa River.

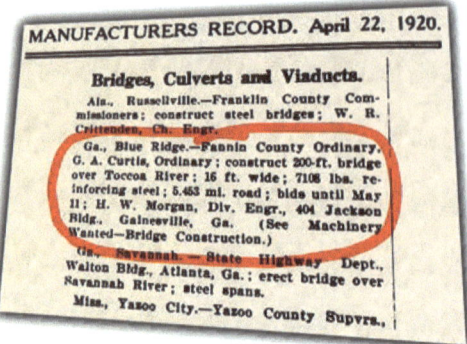

This was before Blue Ridge Lake existed - back then the Toccoa River ran free all the way to the Tennessee state line where it became the Ocoee River.

From the the original 1920 blueprints, the main span of the new bridge was to be 16 feet wide and 150 feet long - in an engineering style known as a "Steel Pratt Truss". The blue prints also show the path the Blue Ridge to Blairsville Highway would take. After leaving the town of Blue Ridge, the road headed east towards and over the Toccoa River where the site of the new bridge was to be constructed. The new steel bridge was just south of an existing covered bridge and road.

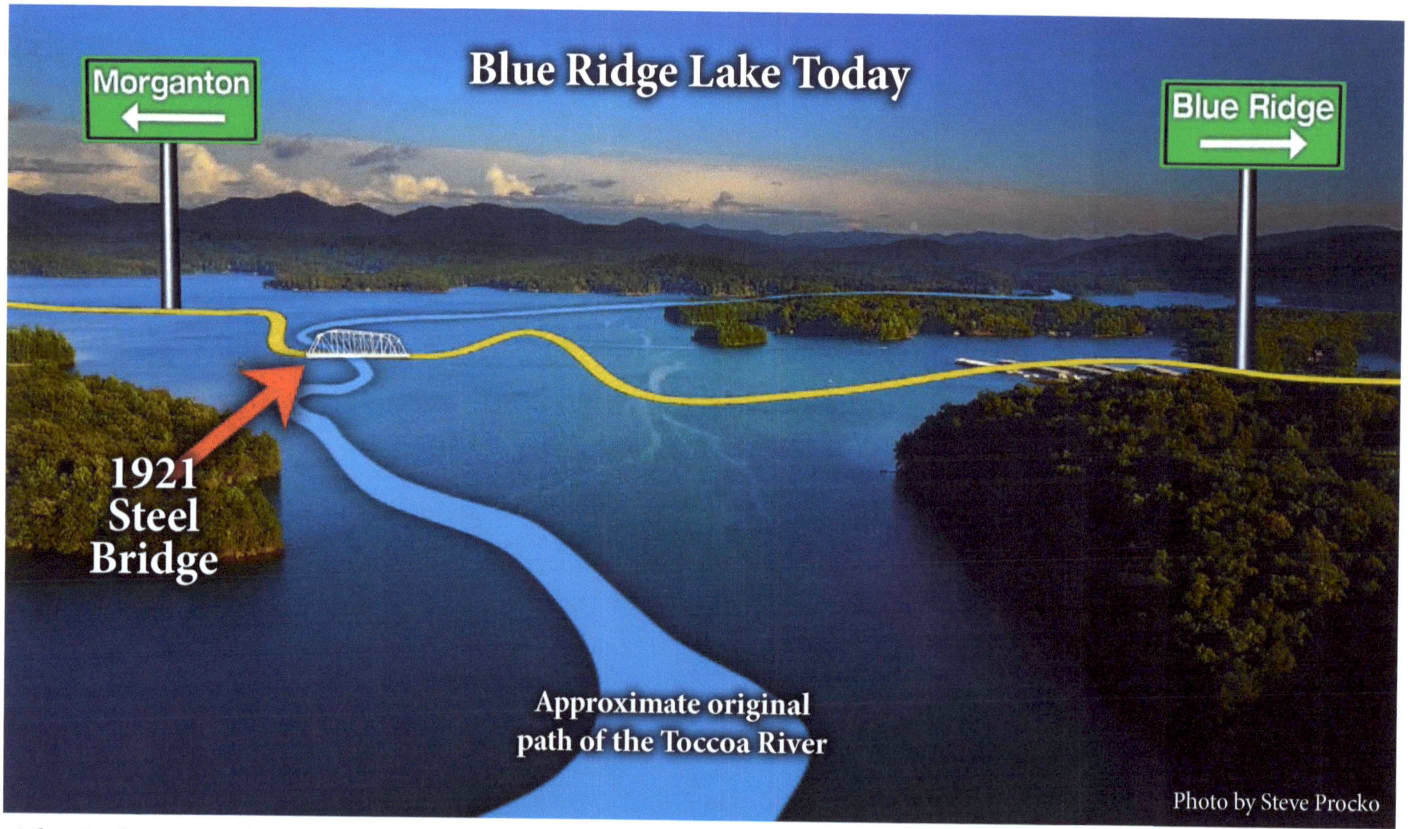

Blue Ridge Lake Today

Morganton ←

Blue Ridge →

1921 Steel Bridge

Approximate original path of the Toccoa River

Photo by Steve Procko

This is the approximate original path in 1921 of the Toccoa River before the lake existed showing where the steel bridge was first constructed. "The Blue Ridge to Blairsville Highway" crossed near Lake Blue Ridge Marina and continued east to Morganton Point and then through the town of Morganton.

Avery Craig

Courtesy of the Craig Family

**Circa 1921 - Construction of the steel bridge began in 1920
and was completed in 1921 along what was called the Blue Ridge to Blairsville Highway.**

The road would have passed by Blue Ridge Marina and run across the lake emerging at Morganton Point. The bridge's construction was a federal aid project that began sometime in late 1920 and was completed in 1921.

From 1920 through 1921, the workers who built this bridge hailed from all over Fannin County. One workman was George Avery Craig (1899-1972), who went by Avery, seen posing on a steel beam at the tallest point in the the bridge construction photo. Craig walked six miles from his home, which was located near present-day Loving Road, back-and-forth to the job site each day while construction took place.

On January 1, 1922, the 4th annual report of the Georgia State Highway Board was published featuring a photo of the completed new bridge over the Toccoa River.

At some point near the end of construction of the steel bridge in 1921, an amazing sight would have presented itself - two bridges, almost right next to each other, crossing the Toccoa River. The older covered bridge rising high above the river, balanced on piers in the river channel and the modern steel replacement bridge to its south.

But this amazing sight would have been short-lived as the covered bridge would soon be torn down. The older covered bridge dated back to at least 1896 when it appears on the US geological survey map for the area.

One person who knew that covered bridge well was Bana O. Kincaid (1898-1996), who lived in Blue Ridge and went to boarding school in Morganton. Bana recounted years later that her father Joseph would take her to school in a horse and wagon. Commenting that both she and the horse disliked going over the rickety old covered bridge because it climbed so high over the Toccoa, it made both the horse and Bana nervous.

Bana O. Kincaid

33

1922 Georgia State Highway Board's very first photo of the completed bridge over the Toccoa River

Rural communities at the time needed electricity, so around the time that the steel bridge was being built, plans were also being made for a new hydroelectric dam to harness the Toccoa River's power, along with a reservoir to be called Lake Toccoa. Construction was soon underway by the Toccoa Electric Company, a subsidiary of the Tennessee Electric Power Company (TEPCO).

At some point as construction of the dam was underway, it was realized that the recently-completed steel bridge was located smack-dab in the middle of where the lake would be. If it wasn't moved, it would soon be submerged under more than 100 feet of water once the area was flooded. Since the bridge was partially built with federal dollars, it could not be left in place and flooded over when the dam was completed.   TEPCO had noted as early as July 1924 that the steel span would need to be salvaged and used elsewhere. In November 1924, TEPCO considered using the steel truss over the new dam's spillway. But the span was too short, and would have required a second span to suit their needs, so the plan was abandoned.

Other issues slowed construction of the dam through the 1920s, but by 1930 it finally approached completion, with no real solution as to what to do with the bridge.

Could it really be possible that they would just let a relatively brand new bridge built with federal dollars be submerged under a lake? Not likely!

On September 16, 1930, a call for bids was published in the *Atlanta Constitution* due just five days later. The fast-track project was to dismantle the bridge over the Toccoa River, and work had to be completed quickly. Everything needed to be done by

October 15, 1930 when the bridge site would begin to be flooded. The article also noted, the bridge would be re-erected at another site.

Eleven days later, The Blue Ridge Summit-Post reported on the progress: "the highway bridge over the Toccoa River above the dam was currently being torn down."

Avery Craig, one of the men who had built the bridge nine years before, was also on the crew that took the bridge apart. He told his son Arlus, "the bridge's rivet heads were chiseled off when they disassembled it."

The bridge was not left at its original site and then flooded by the lake beginning in October 1930. It was disassembled and taken apart like a giant erector set, then it was stored somewhere near Blue Ridge until they could come up with a plan to reuse the bridge.

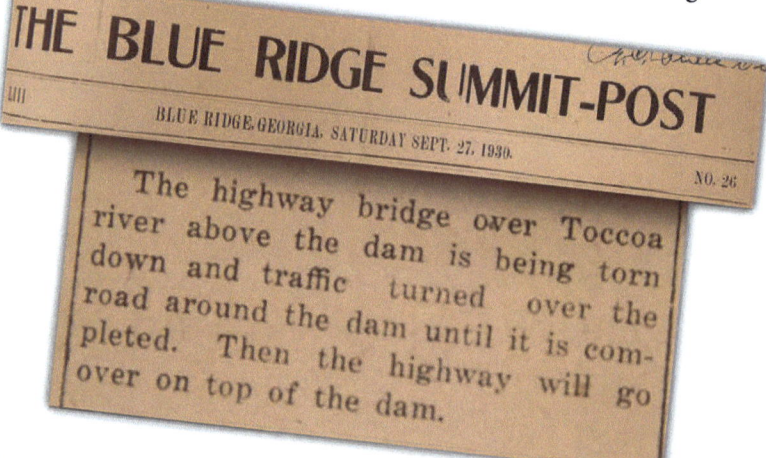

THE BLUE RIDGE SUMMIT-POST

BLUE RIDGE, GEORGIA, SATURDAY SEPT. 27, 1930.   NO. 26

The highway bridge over Toccoa river above the dam is being torn down and traffic turned over the road around the dam until it is completed. Then the highway will go over on top of the dam.

Now we come to the mysterious floating bridge story, which claims that when they were ready to flood the lake, they floated the bridge downstream all the way to McCaysville.

Charles F. Humphrey's (1925-2012) family home sat right on the river where today's Fannin County Visitor's Center now stands. Humphrey claimed to have witnessed the fully intact bridge floating into McCaysville on the Toccoa River, approximately twelve miles downstream from where it was first built, as a 5 year old boy in 1930. "I saw the bridge float on by", recalled Humphrey more than fifty years later with a glint in his eye.

Deep down, you just want to believe that Humphrey's account is true. But facts are funny things.

There are multiple reasons why Humphrey's floating bridge story was impossible, though it must be said, it's a makes for a really great tall-tale, and Charles loved a tall tale.

1921 Steel Bridge

Blue Ridge to Blairsville Highway

Central support pier and approach ramp of earlier covered bridge

Toccoa River

Blue Ridge dam's penstock appears to the left in the foreground. 4,000 yards away the steel bridge is barely visible as well as the remains of the road approach and central piers where the covered bridge once stood. The steel bridge would continue to be used at this location for four more years until October 1930.

about the 'Magical Mystery Steel Bridge'.

Watch a YouTube video

Why was it not possible to float the bridge from where it was first built on the Toccoa downriver to McCaysville/Copperhill?

First - The logistics. A large crane would need to be located and strategically placed in or alongside the Toccoa River in order to lift an intact 7,106+ pound steel bridge onto a barge. Then there was the barge itself, needing to be over 150 feet long to hold the bridge. There were also the clearance obstacles along the way that said barge with said bridge would need to be able to float underneath. At the time, there were at least three bridges located north along the twelve miles between the bridge's original location and Mc-Caysville: Hogback Bend Bridge, the adjacent Mineral Bluff spur bridge of the Louisville and Nashville (L&N) railroad, with its very narrow support piers, and a second L&N railroad bridge just outside of Mc-Caysville.

Second - The river. In 1930, Georgia was experiencing one of the worst droughts in its history. The Toccoa River water levels would have been very low - and a barge loaded with a bridge would have been very heavy. Have you ever tubed down the Toccoa when the river is low? You tend to "bottom out" when the body part hanging out from under the tube meets a river rock. It's the crutial "bottom to river bottom" flotation ratio.

Third - The dam. The most damming argument as to why the bridge was not floated downriver to Mc-Caysville is the actual dam itself. In October 1930, dam construction was complete and they began holding back the Toccoa to flood the region and create the lake. So the dam itself would have been the biggest obstacle of any 150 foot long, 7,106+ pound bridge-loaded barge trying to head downriver.

The facts are, the bridge was disassembled and stored somewhere near Blue Ridge until they could come up with a plan to re-use the bridge.

When the area was flooded in late 1930, creating Toccoa Lake (later rename Blue Ridge Lake in 1934 by Governor Eugene Talmadge) another great magical story was born. Some folks reported actually seeing the bridge going under water as the lake was flooded.

Why did so many people claim they saw the water rise and cover the bridge when they first flooded the lake?

Southeast View
1921 Steel Bridge Over Toccoa

Side-sonar imagery made in 2019 of the original approaches, rails and abutments still in place more than 100' under Blue Ridge Lake.

In fact, leftover parts of the bridge actually did get flooded. They took all of the bridge's steel, but left the concrete. The abutments, east and west approaches, and steel railings on the approaches were all left in place.

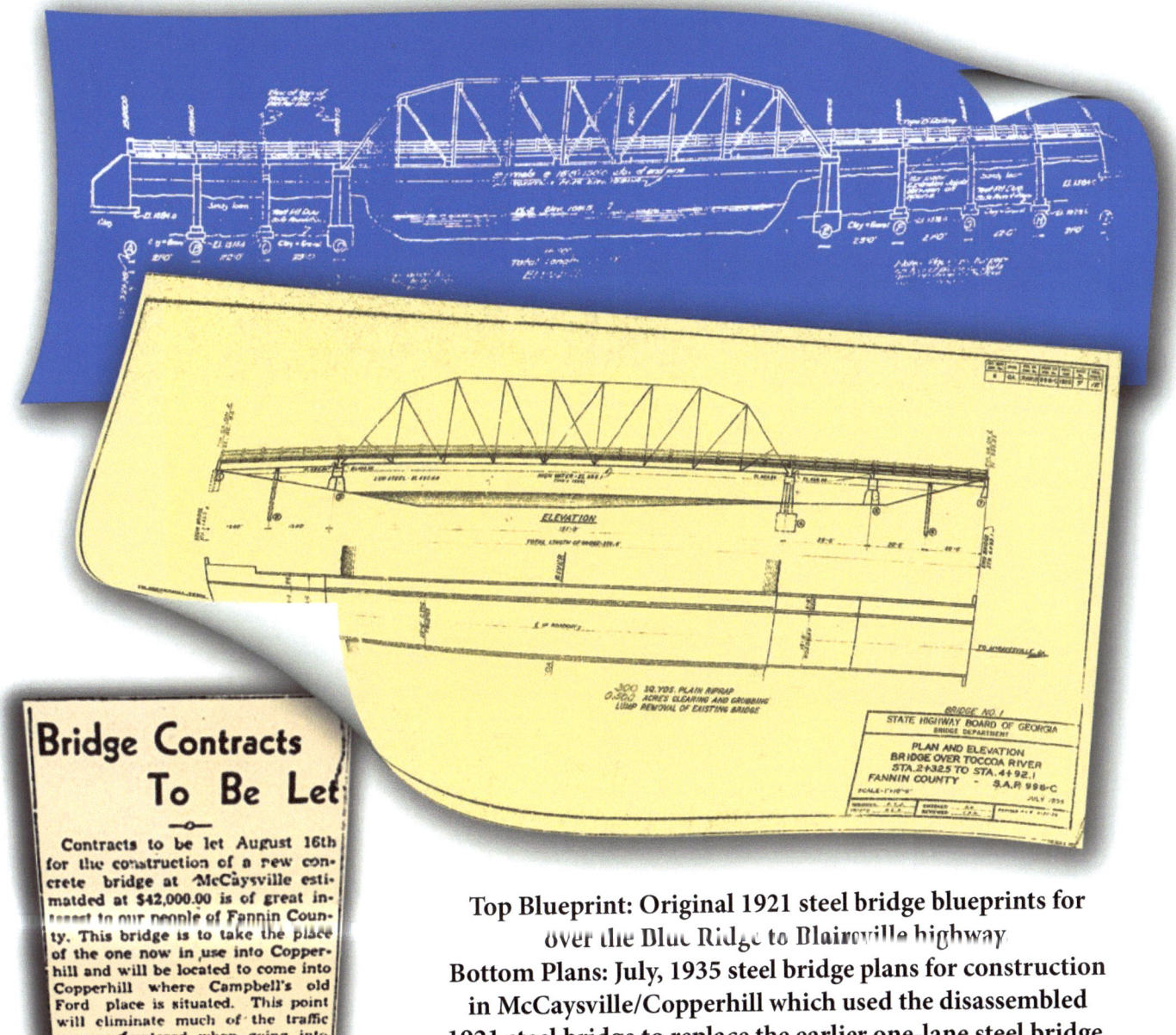

Top Blueprint: Original 1921 steel bridge blueprints for over the Blue Ridge to Blairsville highway

Bottom Plans: July, 1935 steel bridge plans for construction in McCaysville/Copperhill which used the disassembled 1921 steel bridge to replace the earlier one-lane steel bridge.

Bridge Contracts To Be Let

Contracts to be let August 16th for the construction of a new concrete bridge at McCaysville estimated at $42,000.00 is of great interest to our people of Fannin County. This bridge is to take the place of the one now in use into Copperhill and will be located to come into Copperhill where Campbell's old Ford place is situated. This point will eliminate much of the traffic now encountered when going into Copperhill.

A contract for approximately $12,000. will be let for the removal of the old bridge from the old Morganton highway over the Toccoa River to be used for the bridge now is use between McCaysville and Copperhill. This bridge was in use only a few years and will be a great improvement over the one now in use.

Advertisements for these contracts will be found elsewhere in this week's paper.

If you were standing at a distance looking at where the bridge had been as the waters rose, it might look like the bridge itself was going under water. Those leftover bridge parts remain under more than 100 feet of water today, In 2019 they were found using side-scanning sonar.

On August 1, 1935, it was reported in the *Fannin County Times* newspaper that "Bridge Contracts To Be Let" for construction of a new concrete bridge in McCaysville estimated at $42,000. The idea was to improve the traffic pattern through McCaysville and Copperhill, which ran in a serpentine fashion through town over the 1911 single-lane steel bridge. It must have been very challenging driving this route in a large truck, and then manuevering over the bridge and it's ramps.

Also reported in the article was that an approximate $12,000 contract would be provided to move a certain steel bridge that had been stored elsewhere for five years, and that used to be on "the old Morganton highway over the Toccoa River". The plan was to use that bridge to replace an older bridge that spanned the Toccoa between McCaysville and Copperhill. "This bridge was in use for only a few years and will be a great improvement over the one now in use," the newspaper commented.

Blueprints and surveys were taken, and in the GDOT archives today, the entire batch of plans used in 1935 also included the plans from the 1921 Blue Ridge to Blairsville Highway bridge design and construction.

Another drawing showed exactly what the 1921 bridge would look like once it was rebuilt in its new McCaysville/Copperhill digs.

Circa 1936 - The steel bridge was rebuilt at its present-day location over the Toccoa River at McCaysville/Copperhill.

The concrete bridge was completed first, to allow traffic to flow unimpeded through the two towns on a straighter path. Then the original 1921 steel bridge's components were hauled into town by truck and reconstructed at the location it currently occupies.

In the blueprints for the plan, in addition to all the details necessary to convert the bridge's design into its new home, are the additional instructions for the "lump sum removal of the old bridge."

So what became of the 1911 bridge?

Like the rest of this case, the details weren't actually recorded anywhere, and most of the eyewitnesses to the event are long gone. With no great fanfare, first steel bridge was taken apart and stacked on the shore of the river.

At the time, everyone was excited by the idea of getting a new-ish bridge. It was two lanes wide! No more backing down the steep ramps when you met an oncoming car or truck. Little attention was paid as to what happened to the old one. So it is likely it was just unceremoniously scrapped.

On the steel bridge today there's a metal badge mounted to one of its supports on its northwest side that contains the number/letter combination "998-C".

It's the badge of honor added to the structure - the project number for its reconstruction in 1936. The McCaysville/Copperhill steel bridge - more than a century old - a mystery no more - though definitely a heritage landmark that's magical - and that's a fact!

Photo by Steve Procko

The first steel bridge.

The second steel bridge today.
— Photo by Kathy Thompson

Side by side comparison from the same point-of-view more than 100 years apart.

The first 1911 steel bridge is on the left in a photograph made between 1912 and 1925, the second steel bridge, and current bridge, is on the right in this photograph taken from almost the same angle in 2024. The current steel bridge was built elsewhere in 1921, disassembled in 1930, and then rebuilt in 1936 in McCaysville/Copperhill on it current location replacing the first steel bridge.

Of particular note is the height of the first bridge. The approach ramps placed the first bridge significantly higher than the current bridge. It would have been a lot more secure when the Toccoa River flooded. Additionally, the first bridge was narrower and likely a single lane bridge. Interestingly, historian and author Robert E. Barclay wrote in his book "The Copper Basin 1890-1963" that the first steel bridge as a "steel wagon bridge". And although he mentions the construction of the concrete bridge one block over in 1936, he makes no mention of the second steel bridge replacing the first one shortly after the concrete bridge was completed.

Besides both bridges spanning the Toccoa, the history of the two bridges now spans more than 110 years.

Circa 1911-1925

Today

Photo by Kathy Thompson

Acknowledgements

Lane Bishop
Melissa Procko Delahoz
Larry Dyer
Michael Eaton
Harriet Frye
Joe Griffin
Joy Hardin
Dick Hillman
Ray Leader
Karen Hodges Miller
Wilds Pierce

Blue Ridge
Scenic Railway

Ducktown Basin
Museum

Fannin County
Heritage Foundation

L&N Collection,
University of Louisville
Archives

Library of Congress

The Atlanta-Journal
Constitution

The Federal Highway
Administration

Georgia Department of
Transportation

Tennessee Valley
Authority

TEPCO Archives;
Courtesy of the
Chattanooga
Pubic Library

Office of the Clerk
of the Superior Court;
Fannin County

About The Authors

Steve Procko

An Emmy award-winning film-maker and photographer with a love for history. Author Steve Procko particularly loves learning about the small, everyday events in the lives of little-known people and the small towns they lived in.

His first book, **Rebel Correspondent** told the true story of the everyday life of a lowly cavalry private struggling to survive one of the greatest events in American history.

His second book, **Captured Freedom** offered Steve a chance to go on a great scavenger hunt, pinning down the facts about a more than 150-year-old Civil War prisoner-of-war photograph, whose story had been lost to the ethers.

Kathy Thompson

Kathy Thompson moved to Fannin County in 1971 to teach art. Thirty-seven years later she retired and began writing books about the area. Since then, she has written four books, produced another volume for Wilds Pierce (founder of the Blue Ridge Scenic Railway), and wrote **The Tate House Mansion** for the owner Marsha Mann.

The focus of all of these volumes has been regional history, and Appalachian culture, covering an area that includes mountain areas in North Carolina, Eastern Tennessee, and North Georgia. Thompson holds a Doctorate in Arts Education and Creative Thinking from the University of Georgia.

CapturedFreedom.com

KathyThompsonBooks.com

RebelCorrespondent.com

For further information visit HistoryBend.org

Courtesy of the Michael Eaton